George McKinnon Wrong

The Crusade of MCCCLXXXIII., Known as That of the Bishop of Norwich

George McKinnon Wrong

The Crusade of MCCCLXXXIII., Known as That of the Bishop of Norwich

ISBN/EAN: 9783337220105

Printed in Europe, USA, Canada, Australia, Japan

Cover: Foto ©Lupo / pixelio.de

More available books at **www.hansebooks.com**

THE CRUSADE OF

MCCCLXXXIII.,

KNOWN AS THAT OF

THE BISHOP OF NO[RWICH]

BY

WRONG

[SO]UTHAMPTON-STREET, STRAND, LONDON;

AND 27 BROAD-STREET, OXFORD.

1892.

PRINTED BY JAMES PARKER AND CO.,
CROWN YARD, OXFORD.

PREFACE.

THE war-cry of the Crusades in their earlier and better days aroused the generous enthusiasm of thousands to rescue the Cross from its Eastern slavery. But the best impulses of mankind have usually been made the instruments of designing selfishness. The war-cry became in time a political tool, and lost its moral power. Many attempts were made to revive it, and in this little volume the story of one of these is told. The scene is not the distant and mysterious East, but commonplace Flanders; and the Cross is not arrayed against the Standard of the Prophet but against the Cross carried by schismatic hands. The material for the story is scattered, and when it is not scanty it is untrustworthy in its detail. While I have been working upon it a sceptical friend has said to me repeatedly, "We know nothing about the past." I am convinced that he is wrong. The scattered records are fragments broken from the great whole. A thick coating of mistake and passion often covers them, and it is difficult to separate the error from the truth; but sound historical science working from its knowledge of human nature which has remained unchanged, can recall with accuracy, if not with completeness, the vivid life of a past time if it has even scanty contemporary records.

The contents of this book were at first intended to form part of a larger work on the history of England in the latter part of the fourteenth century. Circumstances have made necessary the immediate publication of this portion of it. The notes are inserted as guaranty and proof of statements made. They are intended for the use of special students; others may safely ignore them.

OXFORD,
September 2, 1892.

CONTENTS.

I. THE CONFLICT AT ROME.   PAGE

Death of Gregory XI.—Election of Urban VI.—His quarrel with the Cardinals—The Schism—Rejection of Clement VII., the Antipope, by England—Urban VI. proclaims a Crusade against the Schismatics 1

II. THE BISHOP OF NORWICH.

His ancestry—His early career—Made Bishop of Norwich—His character—Riot at Lynn—Quarrel with St. Alban's Abbey—Suppresses rebels—Appointed to lead the Crusade . . . 10

III. ENGLAND AND FLANDERS.

The two Crusades—The state of Flanders—The position of Ghent—The capture of Bruges—The Count of Flanders' appeal to France—Van Artevelde's appeal to England—The discussion in Parliament—The Battle of Roosebeke . . 18

IV. THE WORK IN THE ENGLISH PARISHES.

The Crusade proclaimed in England—The Bishop of Norwich takes the Cross—The offer of Indulgences—The Church's System of Discipline—The Church's support of the Crusade—The Parish Priest—The Monk—The Friar—The Campaign of the Friars—Wycliffe's opposition—The Friars' success 26

CONTENTS.

V. THE SETTING OUT.

Affairs in Flanders—The Meeting of Parliament—Opposition of Party of John of Gaunt—The Grant to the Bishop of Norwich—The gathering of the Army—The chief officers—The final arrangements—The Bishop crosses to Calais . 45

VI. THE CAMPAIGN IN FLANDERS.

The delay at Calais—The materials for the history—Attack upon and capture of Gravelines—The defeat of the Bastard of Flanders—The Conquest of West Flanders—The effect of the victories in England—The siege of Ypres—The advance of a French army—Final assault of Ypres—The siege raised—The retreat—Calverley abandons Bergues 55

VII. THE END OF THE WAR.

John of Gaunt gathers an army—King Richard's ride—The Royal Council—The siege of Bourbourg—Distress of the French—A truce—Withdrawal from Bourbourg—Gravelines destroyed—The Bishop returns to England—Accused in Parliament—His defence and sentence—Truce with France—The effect of the Crusade . . 81

APPENDIX 92

INDEX 95

I.

THE CONFLICT AT ROME.

VOLTAIRE once said of the Holy Roman Empire that it was nothing that it professed to be. It was neither Holy nor Roman nor an Empire. It would be perhaps too unjust to say that the Crusade of 1383 was based upon an equally barren theory to which it conformed as little, although the war that claimed to be holy did not justify its title. It was modelled upon those greater Crusades, the mention of which calls up a romantic picture of war between the East and the West. These Crusades had, however, been dead for a hundred years, and the one the English made on behalf of Pope Urban VI. in 1383 was only a campaign in Flanders.

Pope Gregory XI. died at Rome on March 27, 1378. Turbulent Rome was more than usually turbulent at the time of his death. Seventy-three years earlier Pope Clement V. had set what the Romans regarded as the bad fashion of a Pope living away from Rome and from Italy. The devoted adherent of the King of France, he took up his residence at Avignon in Provence, so near the French territory as to be under French control, and did not even visit Rome as Pope. His example proved enduring. For two generations the Romans scarcely saw the Holy Father, whose claim to the reverence of Christendom was based upon his succession to the Roman See. Nor was their loss only a spiritual one. The Pope's Court was a centre to which multitudes thronged. Embassies and deputations, pilgrims and travellers came, and the devout brought a more material good than their prayers. Without the Pope Rome was a provincial city torn by faction; with him in her midst, the factions did not disappear, but the city took Imperial rank. To this day, however hostile to the political claims of the Papacy the Roman may be, he is proud that his city is the home of a power so august and universal. But the freer movement of modern life has weakened local sentiment. It was intense at Rome when Gregory XI. died.

With the Pope dead in their midst the Romans saw that their opportunity had come, and they acted promptly. They stationed guards at the city gates and bridges, that the Cardinals should not hurry away and elect Gregory's successor in some other place. Sixteen of the twenty-three Cardinals who then formed the sacred College were in Rome, and it would be the Romans' fault if every effort was not made to secure a Pope who should remember his duty to Rome and to Italy. The chief officers of the city waited upon the Cardinals to urge that a Roman, or at least an Italian, should be chosen, and for the ten days between the death of Gregory and the election of his successor every resource of public and private influence was used to accomplish the desired end. Eleven of the sixteen Cardinals were French, four were Italian, one was Spanish, and the Avignon Captivity had established the tradition of subservience to France.

On the evening of April 7, 1378, the great square of St. Peter's was thronged with a crowd intensely interested in the Papal election which should take place on the following morning in the adjoining Vatican Palace. It was with difficulty that the Chamber in which the Cardinals were to pass the night was cleared of the crowd which had thronged in. At last the Cardinals were left alone, but their rest was disturbed. The people in the square kept up a tumult throughout the night. At daybreak the campanile of St. Peter's was broken open, and the clanging bells summoned a greater crowd. The shouts which penetrated even to the ears of the Cardinals inside the Palace were "A Roman, A Roman! We wish a Roman, or at least an Italian, for Pope!" When they went to Mass in the morning the shouts were so loud that they could scarcely hear the service.

It is difficult to say what effect the tumult of the populace had upon the minds of the Cardinals. Probably it convinced them that delay was impossible, and so curtailed the usual intrigues and negotiations. The result was that a rapid compromise was effected. A man was chosen who had not been the candidate of any of the rival factions, and his election, after some delay, was announced to the people.

Bartolommeo Prignano, Archbishop of Bari, the

new Pope, had been hitherto known as a man of austere life and of considerable executive ability. He was an Italian, but not a Roman, and the announcement of his election excited the fierce wrath of the Roman populace. Concealment alone saved the new Pope's life, but on the following day the Romans were of a better mind. They forgave the failure to elect a Roman when they remembered that they had secured an Italian. The Pope was crowned as Urban VI. on Easter Sunday, April 18, 1378, and the Cardinals at Rome wrote on the following day to their brethren at Avignon announcing the election, and declaring that it had been made freely and unanimously.

But a new storm was brewing. Urban, on the day after his Coronation, rebuked some of the prelates and bishops then in Rome for leaving their Dioceses and neglecting their duties, and the rebukes were not in mild terms. Fourteen days later he publicly and bitterly reproached the Cardinals for their immoral lives, and he denounced the simony that they and so many others high in office in the Church practised. The Cardinals were dismayed. They had hoped that a Pope, elevated suddenly from a much lower rank, would respect the dignity and the opinions of men whom he had long regarded as superiors. They found that they had a contemptuous master who exaggerated his authority. It was ruffling to Cardinal Orsini's dignity to be called, as Urban once called him point blank, a fool, and the other Cardinals did not escape insult. Urban would interrupt their remarks with such comments as "Rubbish," "Hold your tongue." He had indeed moral zeal, but his manners were intolerable.

The two darling wishes of a majority of the Cardinals were that the Papal Court should return to Avignon and that the Papacy should continue subservient to France. The Cardinals were prisoners in whatever place the Pope held his court, and they enjoyed the luxury of Avignon while they dreaded the semi-barbarism of Rome. It was not strange also that a body of men, for the most part French, should favour the policy of the King of France. Urban, however, had no intention of complying with either wish. He announced that he should take up his residence in Rome, and hoped to die there, and he soon declared his intention to create new Roman and Italian Cardinals, and thus to destroy the French majority.

This announcement brought the disputes between him and his Cardinals to a crisis. Vain efforts to alter the Pope's determination resulted in an open breach. The Cardinals who had meanwhile withdrawn from Urban's court were at last united at Fundi in the early autumn of 1378. On Sept. 18 Urban, who was at Tivoli, created twenty-eight new Cardinals, and thus placed his enemies in the minority. This made prompt action on their part necessary. They declared that Urban's election was invalid because it had been forced upon them by the Roman populace, and that the Papal chair was vacant. On September 20 they proceeded to fill it. Robert of Geneva was chosen, and took the title of Pope Clement VII.

Thus arose the great Schism, from which the Crusade of 1383, known in English history as the Bishop of Norwich's Crusade, sprang. Each Pope had a certain show of right on his side. The supporters of Urban claimed that the Cardinals had not the right to undo what they had the right to do. Urban had been duly elected, and the authority of the Cardinals ended there. On the other side it was urged that there had been no true election. No one could doubt that the crowd outside the Vatican was a threatening crowd, likely to use violent measures if their wishes were not met. The Cardinals had voted under compulsion, and only a free election was valid. History has pronounced in favor of Urban's claims, but the case was in truth a fine one for the lawyers, some of whose contemporary opinions may still be read [1].

Questions, however, which involve large national interests may be influenced but can never be finally determined by legal logic, and it was soon seen

---

[1] The chief authorities consulted for this sketch are :—

Conciliengeschichte von Carl Joseph von Hefele 6ʳ Band (1890), pp. 727—791. Bishop von Hefele gives at length the statements on either side.

Geschichte der Päpste seit dem Ausgang des Mittelalters, von Ludwig Pastor 1ʳ Band (1886), pp. 95—102.

"History of the Papacy during the Reformation," by M. Creighton (now Bishop of Peterborough). Vol. I. (1882), pp. 55—66.

that the nations of Europe would attach themselves to the side that their political desires favoured. Clement was the nominee of France. It was, therefore, quite certain that England, France's foe, would adopt Urban's side. For the Cardinals concerned the question was one that involved something more than spiritual interests. Now-a-days we think of a Dean or Canon of an English Cathedral as an English gentleman holding a position of high dignity in his own land. In the days of the Schism, however, many of the dignitaries of the English Church were Italian ecclesiastics who had never seen England and could not speak a word that should be understood by its people[1]. For some of the rebellious Cardinals the problem in regard to England was a serious financial one. If England joined Urban every penny of their English revenues would be handed over to the rival Pope.

Envoys from both sides came to England, and at a Parliament held at Gloucester in October, 1378, Clement's representatives made an able argument. In vain. "By the will of the Lord God who disposes all things justly the apostate envoys were repulsed," says a St. Alban's Chronicler[2]. The Archbishop of Canterbury preached in public against Clement, or as he was called by Urban's side,

---

[1] The frequent Royal Warrants for the transfer of Church revenues to Pope Urban, or in some cases to other foreign nominees, show how numerous the English benefices thus held were. See Rymer's *Fœdera*, *passim*.

[2] *Chronicon Angliae*, Ed. by E. M. Thompson, R. S., p. 212.

Robert, from the suitable text, "There shall be one Shepherd of all" (Ezek. xxxvii. 24 [1]), and political and ecclesiastical feeling in England led the nation with some enthusiasm to the side of Urban. The Parliament declared forfeit all the revenues of the Cardinals in England, and enacted that persons recognizing anyone but Urban as Pope should be deprived of their goods [2].

The Schism was now irrevocable. Each Pope denounced the other as worse than heathen, and called upon Europe to crusade to suppress the usurper. It is unnecessary for us to follow here the dreary conflict in the wider field. We are concerned only with its effect in England in bringing about the Crusade of 1383. The Schism introduced into international conflicts, already sufficiently bitter, the intensity of religious passion. Englishmen who had hitherto fought Frenchmen on national grounds were now to be exhorted in the terms that the Bishop of Norwich and Sir Hugh Calverley used at Gravelines in the opening fight of the Crusade: "You fight in the cause of God and of the whole Church. Those who die in this cause will be martyrs. There is no less merit in killing such dogs as these (the French and Flemings) than in destroying as many Jews or Saracens [3]."

The Bulls which Pope Urban issued calling the

---

[1] *Chron. Ang.*, p. 212.
[2] 2 Ric. II. Stat. i. c. 7 ("Statutes of the Realm," ii. 11).
[3] *Historia Anglicana*, by Thomas Walsingham. R. S., ii. 89.

English people to his aid are almost frantic in their passion[1]. Yet it would be easy to exaggerate the intensity of feeling which his call to arms excited. The theorizing spirit of the Middle Ages was apt to spend itself in language, and Pope Urban used especially strong language. With his military impotence, language was his only resource, and he must make it go as far as possible. His adherents used similar phrases. Yet we are surprised that it all produced so little effort. The Crusaders were to receive pardon for their sins, and sinners both rich and poor heard the message gladly. The cause called forth its devoted adherents; yet probably no campaign was undertaken that should not have been undertaken on other grounds. It was not really against Robert of Geneva, who falsely called himself Pope Clement VII., that the English fought. The more ignorant or pious may have thought that the war was a holy war. It was convenient that they should think so. But the politicians and the business men of the time knew better. It was against the enemies of English commerce in Flanders and the enemies of English claims in France that the crusading force was arrayed.

[1] See the one in Walsingham, ii. 72—76.

II.

THE BISHOP OF NORWICH.

AMONG the youngest and most active of the English Bishops at this time was Henry Despenser, Bishop of Norwich. He was now about forty years of age, and in 1382, when the movement for the crusade began, had been Bishop of Norwich for twelve years. The ancestry of Despenser was such as to make his military tastes and even his imperious temper quite natural. The first prominent member of the family was Hugh Despenser, Justiciar of England, who, siding with his fellow Barons in the Barons' war, was killed with Simon de Montfort at the Battle of Evesham in 1265[1]. From him to the Bishop of Norwich the family is remarkable for the stormy careers of its chief members. In the direct line during this period every one met with a violent death. The son and grandson of the Justiciar were Hugh Despenser the Elder and Hugh Despenser the Younger, who became the chief advisers of Edward II., and were known by the contemptuous name of 'favorites.' Days of misfortune came for them and for King Edward. The Queen Isabella and Roger Mortimer, Earl of March, drove

---

[1] "Chronicles Edward I. and Edward II." Edited by W. Stubbs. Rolls Series, i. 69.

them into the West and the elder Despenser at last surrendered to the Queen at Bristol, on October 26, 1326. The mob clamoured for his execution, and it took place on the next day. He died the terrible death of a traitor. His bowels were torn out and burned before his eyes; he was then hanged, beheaded, and quartered. Within less than a month his son met with a similar fate at Hereford, and the estates and titles of father and son were declared forfeit [1].

The younger Despenser, who had married Eleanor, sister and co-heiress of Gilbert, Earl of Gloucester, and niece of Edward II., was the Bishop of Norwich's grandfather, so that the Bishop was not remotely connected with the Royal family [2]. The widowed lady appeared before Queen Isabella and her young son Edward III., and pleaded that the property which she had possessed in her own right might be rescued from her husband's forfeited estates. The just claim was granted. Edward III. at a later period exercised a recognized feudal right and married her son Edward to a daughter of Sir Ralph Ferrars, one of his knights, and this Edward Despenser, father of the Bishop of Norwich, also died a violent death. He was killed at the siege of Vannes in 1342, five years after his marriage, when Henry Despenser, the future Bishop, was a mere

---

[1] "Chronicles Edward I. and Edward II." Edited by W. Stubbs. Rolls Series, i. 322; ii. 87—89; 289. Knighton, 2544 and 2547-49; Walsingham, i. 183-5; Froissart, ii. 78—80.

[2] "Chronicles Edward I. and Edward II," i. 292.

infant[1]. We know nothing of the Bishop's youth. His three brothers were all soldiers, but he became at an early age an ecclesiastic and a Canon of Salisbury[2]. His brother Edward was in Froissart's admiring eyes the beau-ideal of a chivalrous Knight[3], and the Canon of Salisbury, although an ecclesiastic, joined him in a campaign in Italy on behalf of Pope Urban V.[4] The elder brother may have performed some distinguished service which claimed the Pope's gratitude, or persistent solicitation on the spot may have proved efficacious. At any rate the valuable appointment to the See of Norwich, then one of the chief cities in England, was given to Henry Despenser before he was thirty years of age[5]. He was consecrated, at Rome it is alleged, on April 20, 1370[6], and returned to England soon after[7], not to forget his camp life but to take meanwhile a prominent part in the work of the Bishops in Parliament[8].

On the Bishop's tomb in Norwich Cathedral were

[1] He was the youngest of four children, and his father had been married five years. Froissart, ii. 106.

[2] Rymer's *Fœdera*, Record Ed., iii. pt. ii. p. 900.

[3] Froissart, ii. 106.

[4] Froissart, vii. 251; x. 210. Capgrave, "Chronicles of England," Rolls Series, 226.

[5] Capgrave, *De Illustribus Henricis*, p. 170.

[6] Le Neve's *Fasti*, ed. by Hardy, ii. 465. Wharton, *Anglia Sacra*, i. 415 n.

[7] He received the spiritualities of his See from the Archbishop of Canterbury, July 12, 1370 (Wharton, as above), and the temporalities from the King, August 14. (Rymer, iii. pt. ii. 900.)

[8] His name occurs frequently on Committees of Parliament. *Rotul. Parl. passim.*

described various traits of his character, and among them it was told that his morning meditation as his thoughts arose heavenward was, 'The Earth is the Lord's'[1]. This thought interpreted in the spirit of one who was both a mediæval churchman and by his connections a great noble, gives us the key to his character. There is nothing to show that he was lacking in spiritual sincerity, but he mixed his pastoral functions strangely with conflicts about worldly trifles. The Earth was the Lord's, and he was the Lord's agent in the part of the heritage committed to him. Those who tampered with his rights were trifling with what the Lord had established. The defect of the principle was that it encouraged arrogance in the Lord's representative.

A few incidents well illustrate his character. Lynn, an important town in his Diocese, was known later as Lynn Regis or King's Lynn, but it was at the time of which we speak, Lynn Episcopi or Bishop's Lynn. The Bishops of Norwich were over-lords of the town. The practise at Lynn was that when the Mayor went through the streets in procession he was preceded by a mace-bearer with the civic staff, but custom had not granted this honor to the Bishops of Norwich.

In 1377 Despenser visited Lynn as Bishop, and when the procession was being formed in his honor, demanded to have the civic staff borne before him. He was lord of the town, and of higher rank than the

[1] Spirat ad astra boni Pastoris mens matutinis dicendo "Domini est terra." Capgrave, *De Illustribus Henricis*, Rolls Series, 174.

Mayor. The aldermen said it would be dangerous to do it. The people were evilly disposed already, and would resent the innovation, and might kill those granting it. The Bishop, however, insisted. He would do what he wished even if the ribald mob did not like it. He was surprised at the cowardice of the aldermen, and their fear of the common people, who were, he said, of no account [1]. The aldermen begged that they at any rate might be excused from the procession, and the Bishop started, one of his own company bearing the staff. It was now growing dark. The alarm spread among the people. They closed the town gates and attacked the Bishop. He and his horse and some of his company were wounded, and there was a very lively disturbance which required royal intervention before it was finally settled [2].

In another case the Bishop asserted his rights against privileged ecclesiastics. Three years after the fight at Lynn he had a dispute with the powerful Abbey of St. Alban's. A recent Convocation had granted to the King a tax of one-tenth on the clergy. The Bishop of Norwich ordered the Prior of Wymundham, a Priory in his Diocese belonging to the Abbey of St. Alban's, to do the distasteful work of

---

[1] His tone was that of the dominant class of the time towards the common people. "Faceret quae proposuerat, invitis communibus, quos ribaldos vocabat. Objurgavit etiam majores cives villae de pusillanimitate sua, eo quod dixerant se timere vulgus villae, quos pro nihilo ipse ducebat." *Chron. Ang.*, 140.

[2] Rymer, vii. 157. The story is told in *Chron. Ang.*, 139, 140.

collecting the tax. The Prior pleaded that he was exempt from such a duty, and that only his superior, the Abbot of St. Alban's or the Pope, could require it of him. But the Bishop insisted upon his demand, and thus brought on another conflict about his rights. This time the weapons were those of the law, and the Bishop lost his case, much to the joy of the St. Albans' monk who tells the story [1].

His martial spirit was his most distinguishing trait. When the Peasants' Revolt reached Norfolk in 1381, John the Lyster, or Dyer, put himself at the head of the movement, and with their singular fascination for the name of King the peasants greeted him as "King of the Common People" (Rex Communium). For a short time the Dyer ruled with the arrogance if not with the dignity of a king. He forced the knights whom he had seized to serve him on bended knee at table. But his glory was short-lived. The rebels soon saw that pardon must be procured, and in order to command attention to their claims they sent two of the captured knights, Sir William de Morley and Sir John Brewes, to the King, accompanied by three of the leaders in the revolt, Sceth, Trunch, and Cubith [2].

The company started on their journey. Meantime the Bishop of Norwich, while staying at his manor of Burleigh, near Stamford, had heard of the revolt. He had taken the road at once, arrayed in complete armour and with a small band of eight

---

[1] *Chronicon Angliae*, 258—261.
[2] Capgrave gives their names. *De Illustribus Henricis*, p. 171.

lances and a few archers, and soon fell in with the little company of delegates at Icklingham, not far from Newmarket. The rebels were at once seized. Despenser said that he as Bishop had the right to punish members of his flock who had forfeited the protection of the King, and condemned them to death. This was bad law, for a well known principle of Ecclesiastical law forbids clerics to inflict the death penalty. But the three men were promptly beheaded [1], and their heads were sent to be exposed at Newmarket. The Bishop hurried on to North Walsham, where the rebel force was entrenched. His decision dispelled the panic of the loyal portion of the populace, and he attacked the rebel camp with a large force. In the hand-to-hand fight which followed the Bishop was everywhere "like a wild boar gnashing with his teeth, sparing neither himself nor his enemies." The rebels were routed, and John the Lyster was taken. The Bishop, continuing to act upon the legal principles he had already laid down, condemned him to be hanged, drawn, and quartered. But the chief pastor did not forget his spiritual functions. The condemned man's judge murmured spiritual consolations to him, and confessed and absolved him. When John was being dragged to the scaffold in the cruel fashion of the times, the Bishop supported his head lest it should strike the ground, "discharging in this," says

---

[1] The third had gone off to buy food, but according to Capgrave was also executed by the Bishop. *De Illustribus Henricis*, 171.

an admiring monk, "a work of clemency and piety [1]." We are almost justified in saying that the Bishop was maddened by the taste of blood. He marched from Norfolk into Cambridge and Huntingdonshires to crush the risings there. The terrified rebels fled to the Churches for sanctuary. But the Church could not protect them against the Church's avenger. They were struck down with swords and spears at the altar itself. The Bishop spared none. Our informant, a monk of Leicester, rejoices that his hand was stretched out wide in vengeance, and that the rebels received only the absolution of the sword [2].

Shortly after this the Bishop was appointed by Pope Urban VI. to a work that should carry him farther afield. The news of his late military exploits had perhaps reached Rome, or possibly the Bishop saw and sought an opportunity for distinguishing himself. In any case he seemed admirably fitted by temper and reputation for the work of the Crusade to which he was now summoned.

[1] The whole story is in *Chronicon Angliae*, 304-8. The rebels quite understood that it was the Bishop who had crushed them, and in the next year made a plot to murder him and others. (Ibid., 354.)

[2] Higden, 2638-9.

III.

ENGLAND AND FLANDERS.

IN 1382, probably in the summer, Pope Urban's Bull reached England [1], appointing the Bishop of Norwich to lead a crusade against the Schismatics. The Antipope and his adherents, wherever found, constituted the generous range of adversaries whom he might attack. The Pope's intention, however, was that there should be more than one crusade. The reigning King of Castile was an adherent of the Antipope. John of Gaunt, Duke of Lancaster, King Richard's uncle, claimed the throne of Castile on behalf of his wife Constance, daughter of Pedro the Cruel, King of Castile; and John of Gaunt held to Pope Urban. So now the Pope gave him his blessing, and called upon him to crusade for his crown [2]. The Bishop's crusade was the more flexible, and could be adapted to the most pressing want of the time. John of Gaunt's was for a special and indeed a personal and selfish end, and the English people did not so love John of Gaunt that they were ready

---

[1] The contents of the Bull were well known in England by the autumn. See *Rot. Parl.*, iii. 134, 140.

[2] *Rot. Parl.*, iii. 133, 134. *Historia Vitae et Regni Ricardi II.*, by a Monk of Evesham, Ed. by Hearne, p. 41.

to make any sacrifices on his account. It followed that in the autumn of 1382, when the proposed crusades were being discussed, a strong public opinion was forming in favor of the Bishop of Norwich as against John of Gaunt. The King had not yet formally approved either crusade, and until he did so the active work could not begin. Meanwhile the relations of England to France and Flanders became such that the mind of the nation turned to the crusade of the Bishop of Norwich as the best means of helping England in a time of great difficulty.

Froissart, himself a native of Valenciennes, laments the ceaseless troubles of Flanders at this time. The country was the market-place of Europe, and the state in which the rich people of the towns lived was surprising in its magnificence. But there was envy and strife, and Ghent fought Bruges, and Bruges fought Ghent, and the other towns followed their bad example. The great conflict, however, was between the lord of the country, the Count of Flanders, and the towns whose liberties he attempted to restrict. When Froissart sought a reason for the bloodshed and ruin in a land that might have enjoyed peace and riches, he could only come to the probably just conclusion that the Devil was the cause of all the discord [1].

Of the towns of Flanders, Ghent was the largest,

---

[1] *Chroniques de Froissart*, ix. 158, 159: Ce fu oevre de diable; car vous savés ou vous avés oy dire les sages que li diables soutille et atisse nuit et jour à bouter guerre et hainne là où il voit païs.

the most powerful, and the most turbulent. It was the chief seat of the woollen manufacture, and had close commercial ties with England, the great wool-producing country. The large artizan and commercial population was animated by a fierce love of liberty, and in the long conflicts with Louis de Male, Count of Flanders, who ruled from 1346 to 1384, Ghent was always the city that held out longest, and to the last she remained unconquered by him, though losing her liberties soon after his death. The fortunes of war had in the spring of 1382 brought Ghent very low. She alone still held out against the Count of Flanders. The city was not actually besieged, but the source of supplies was cut off. No provisions could reach Ghent and famine followed [1], and this at last forced the men of Ghent to send their chief-captain, Philip van Artevelde, son of the more famous patriot James van Artevelde, to try to make terms with the representatives of the Count of Flanders at Tournay. The only terms the Count would consent to were hard enough. All the male inhabitants of the town between the ages of fifteen and sixty must come out to him on the road to Bruges, bare-headed, wearing only their shirts, and with ropes around their necks, that he might hang or spare whom he would [2].

Philip van Artevelde returned to Ghent, summoned a meeting of the citizens, and announced the Count's

---

[1] Froissart, ix. 438—440.　　　[2] Ibid. x. 12.

terrible terms[1]. An impulse of despair seized the people. They would make a last fight for life and liberty. A band of five thousand men was organized and set out for Bruges, where the Count of Flanders lay, in the hope of taking it by a sudden attack. The effort was entirely successful; Bruges fell into their hands, and the Count of Flanders had difficulty in escaping with his life[2]. It was now early in May, 1382. Bruges, after some sacrifices to the vengeance of the men of Ghent, joined the popular cause. Ypres and the other chief towns followed, and soon the situation was reversed. Ghent and her allies held, under Philip van Artevelde, nearly the whole country, and the Count of Flanders was obliged to seek in France the outside support that was necessary if he would regain his power[3].

It was furnished abundantly. Charles VI., the young King of France, a child with a mind prematurely enfeebled, dreamed only of imitating the chivalrous deeds of the tales that he had read; and it suited the policy of his uncles just then to attempt to subdue the democracy of Flanders. The democracy of Paris would receive a useful warning so[4]. In the autumn of 1382 a French army was gathering at Arras to support the Count of Flanders and to crush Philip van Artevelde[5].

[1] Froissart gives a dramatic picture of the meeting, colored no doubt to the reader's taste, x. 15—22.
[2] Ibid. 22—50. [3] Ibid. 62—68.
[4] Kervyn de Lettenhove, *Histoire de Flandre*, iii. 496; Froissart, x. 68—71.
[5] *Religieux de St. Denis.* Ed. by L. Bellaguet, p. 174.

Van Artevelde turned to England. The danger of Flanders was real, and the triumph of England's enemy there meant danger to England. Every motive of self-interest called the English nation to the rescue. The people saw this, and the Flemish envoys were everywhere received cordially by them[1]. Parliament assembled early in October, about the time of the arrival of the envoys[2], and the matter of aid to Flanders was a part of its most important business[3].

Since the Peasants' revolt John of Gaunt was a changed man. The universal detestation in which he was then seen to be held had apparently convinced him that any intrigues of his to gain the Crown would be vain. Henceforth we find him the friend and adviser of Richard II[4]. The reaction against the peasantry had brought favor to their enemy, and John of Gaunt's influence was predominant in the Parliament of October, 1382[5]. Not the young King but John of Gaunt, with the Earls of Buckingham, Salisbury, and other members of the Royal Council, received the Flemish envoys when they presented themselves at the Palace of Westminster[6]. The envoys were unwise enough to couple their appeal for help with a demand for payment of

[1] Froissart, x. 76, 77.
[2] Rymer's *Fœdera*, Original Edition, vii. 367.
[3] *Rot. Parl.*, iii. 132, 133.
[4] Stubbs' "Const. Hist. of Eng.," ii. 485, 6.
[5] This is evident from the whole tone of the proceedings. *Rot. Parl.*, iii. 132–143.
[6] Froissart, x. 79.

a debt of 200,000 crowns[1] which Edward III. had incurred to them forty years before. John of Gaunt and his fellow-councillors looked at each other and smiled when this demand was made, and after the envoys had retired, broke out in adverse criticism of their appeal. "They ask help and demand money too. It is not reasonable that we should both pay and help them[2]." Excuses were made to delay the envoys, and meanwhile there were many altercations in Parliament in regard to the situation[3]. Outside the Parliament many were eager to attack France and support the Flemish towns. The Bishop of Norwich, ready to crusade against the French as adherents of the Antipope, stood as the champion of the national cause. The mercantile interests were on his side, and the Commons petitioned Parliament in his favor. His expedition, they said, should set out first, that of John of Gaunt might come later[4]. Every one agreed that Flanders must be helped, but John of Gaunt pressed his expedition as equally important, and the lay branches of the Parliament who represented the dominant classes rather than the people, favored him. In any event the King must have money. The laity made a grant of a tax of one-fifteenth upon themselves; but the clergy refused to grant the tenth demanded from them. They were dissatisfied with the half-hearted action of the Crown in suppressing the heresy of Wycliffe

[1] 200,000 viés escus. Ibid. 80. [2] Ibid. 81.
[3] Malverne's Continuation of Higden's *Poly-Chronicon*, ix. 14.
[4] *Rot. Parl.*, iii. 140.

and his followers, which was rampant, and they were hostile to the Spanish expedition. The feeling of their order too was for the cause of their own member, the Bishop of Norwich. The Parliament separated without any grant from them, but at Oxford, a month later, they consented to a grant of one tenth on condition that the King should support the Church in the suppression of the Wycliffe heresy [1].

The King now had money, but his Council was in no hurry to come to the help of Flanders. The envoys were sent back to procure fuller powers on the plea that their present ones were inadequate, and so the negotiation ended for the time [2]. But promises of some kind had been given to them, and Philip van Artevelde announced publicly at Ypres that he was expecting a strong English reinforcement immediately [3].

Meanwhile the French who had gathered at Arras advanced on Flanders, and soon carried all before them. Ypres opened its gates [4]. They sacked Poperinghe, and fearing a like fate, Cassel, Bergues, Bourbourg, and other towns in the south of Flanders surrendered, and basely gave up for execution the captains who had led the resistance to the Count of Flanders [5]. Philip van Artevelde, too confident of his strength, determined to stake all on one battle. He

[1] Malverne, Continuation of Higden, ix. 14. *Chronicon Angliae*, 355.
[2] Walsingham, ii. 71. [3] Froissart, x. 111-12.
[4] Froissart, x. 142—146; *Religieux de St. Denis*, 200-2.
[5] Froissart, x. 147, 148. Kervyn de Lettenhove, *Histoire de Flandre*, iii. 518.

took up his position at Roosebeke, on the road between Ypres and Bruges, and here the French attacked him on November 30, 1382. The unskilled Flemish civilians were no match for the chivalry of France. Van Artevelde's army was defeated and almost destroyed, and he himself was killed [1]. Flanders saw another rapid change of masters, and again Ghent stood almost alone. She opened her gates to all refugees, and once more looked to England for help. The triumph of the French was indeed a disaster for the English. The English merchants were expelled from Bruges, and their property was confiscated [2]. Calais even was in danger. The French were at Dunkirk and Gravelines, and might by a sudden dash on Calais drive the English out [3].

[1] *Religieux de St. Denis*, 204—230. Froissart, x. 151—174.
[2] Walsingham, ii. 81.
[3] Malverne's Continuation of Higden, ix. 15.

IV.

THE WORK IN THE ENGLISH PARISHES.

THE battle of Roosebeke brought momentary decision to the wavering Councils of Richard II. Every one saw now that something must be done against the French. The news of the disaster travelled quickly, and within seven days of the battle the King's Council had decided that the Bishop of Norwich's crusade must be pressed forward. On Dec. 6, 1382, the Bishop was ordered to proclaim the Crusade against the Antipope, and soon he was engaged on the active work of enlisting the support and sympathy of the English people [1].

To organize the First Crusade, Pope Urban II. called a Council at Clermont in Auvergne in 1095. The Pope spoke with an eloquence never surpassed in its effect. "Soldiers of Hell," he said to the rude and quarrelsome knights who heard him, "become soldiers of the living God." He held up the Cross: "It is Christ Himself who issues from His tomb, and presents to you His Cross. It will be the sign raised among the nations. Wear it upon your shoulders and upon your breasts; let it shine upon your arms and upon your standards.... It will increasingly remind you that Christ died for you, and that it is your duty to die for Him." Many rushed forward

---

[1] Rymer, vii. 372.

to take the Cross, and all through Europe the cry spread, " Whosoever will not take up his cross and follow Me is not worthy of Me[1]." To take the Cross became for the next two hundred years the seal of the determination to go to the Holy war. But now these Crusades were dead, and the ritual of the ceremony was forgotten.

The Bishop of Norwich, however, wished it to be clearly seen that it was a Crusade he was leading, and he caused a search at all the Cathedrals for the ritual. At last it was found at Westminster Abbey, and a stately service was held at St. Paul's on St. Thomas's Day, December 21, 1382. Instead of the airy freedom of Wren's noble dome there was the forest shade of the Gothic aisle. The Bishop of London officiated, and the Bishop of Norwich took the Cross and made the vows of a Crusader. On the steps before the door of the choir of St. Paul's the cross was erected, and under its shadow no doubt an eloquent sermon was preached, urging zeal for the Crusade to a thronging crowd. The sky was cloudless, but for two days and three nights previously there had been heavy rains followed by disastrous floods. The change was thought to be a happy omen for the good work thus solemnly begun [2].

However much our attention may be diverted by the political character of the Crusade we ought not

---
[1] Von Hefele's *Conciliengeschichte*, v. 226—232; Michaud's " History of the Crusades," Eng. Transl., i. 43—54.
[2] Continuation of Higden, ix. 16.

to forget that it was to the religious hopes and fears of the English people that it appealed. By the Pope's direction the door of every Church, the gate of every monastery, was to have a copy of his Bull posted upon it [1], and the work was to be the work of the Church. The Bishop conceived that the mission entrusted to him was to exterminate and destroy the heretics. Their offices, their property and their liberty were in any case to be taken from them. Those harboring them were to be outcast and excommunicate. The priest who knowingly gave one of them Christian burial could only be absolved after he had exhumed the body with his own hands, and cast it out of Christian ground [2].

But if the denunciations were stern, the promises were enticing. Ever since the Council of Clermont Crusaders had received special indulgence from Penance on earth or in Purgatory, and had been promised the joys of Heaven. The same blessings were extended later to those aiding a Crusade, and now they were offered to a generous variety of persons—to Crusaders, to those sending and paying for a substitute, and to those giving for the work in proportion to their means. The Bishop of Norwich was to estimate what would be a just measure for the last class [3].

The Church's doctrine of Indulgences was and is easily and usually misunderstood even by those con-

---

[1] Walsingham, ii. 72. This indicates that many were able not only to read, but to read Latin.
[2] Ibid. 75, 76, 79.   [3] Ibid. 77, 78.

fiding in them. The Indulgence was not an unconditional pardon of sin, for repentance and confession were always insisted upon. It might suit the preacher to ignore and the sinner to forget this sometimes, but any sound theologian would have explained that the Church promised bliss with such confidence only because she knew that God forgives the contrite in heart [1]. To her belonged the humbler office of vindicating His justice by declaring the penances on earth or in Purgatory required for sin, and days or months or years might be taken from a man's torments, the humiliation of publicly acknowledging and doing penance for his sin might be spared him, if he took the Church's offer of relief when it was made in an Indulgence [2].

Chaucer, who throws so much light upon the life of this period, has not forgotten to touch upon the Church's system of discipline. She could inflict penalties for moral offences, and as these are usually secret their discovery required close watching. A detestable class of Summoners grew up, some of whom made their living by acting as spies or by trumping up offences against those who could pay to

---

[1] See the Form of Absolution, Walsingham, ii. 79, 80:—"The lying accusation of modern days that indulgences and remission of penance for mortal sin could be obtained by money or by any means whatever, by persons impenitent or who still intended to commit a sin, was unknown in the Middle Ages." (Maskell, *Monumenta Ritualia Ecclesiae Anglicanae*, 2 Edw. III. 374.) The statement is too strong. The claim was known but it was not adopted by any careful Church teacher. See Wycliffe's Latin Sermons, iv. 121.

[2] See the indulgence from penance in Maskell, iii. 375, 6.

be let off. It was not strange that those whose sins, if confessed or discovered, involved heavy penance were sometimes glad to get the offered Indulgence. Froissart's sagacious remark is, however, true, that men do not take much account of pardons until face to face with death [1]. The ills we have we can measure and learn to bear, but an uneasy conscience is haunted by fears of what cannot be defined. The Church did not make light of the suffering that sin involves hereafter. She taught that few died so pure but some chastening torments in purgatory were required, and the Indulgence that took this shadow from the spirit of one on the edge of the grave, or relieved those already departed, was a boon to both the living and the dead. The sorrowing mother might find comfort in releasing her dead child, the lover in freeing his dead love. A system dealing with such mysteries did not escape the abuse to which it was peculiarly open. Pardoners with their red-sealed papers "from Rome all hot" had become common [2]. These men often claimed for their wares sudden and miraculous powers to snatch souls from torment, and their extravagance had brought the system into some disrepute. The tenacity of English faith in it was even then re-

---

[1] Il n'eu font trop grant compte fors au destroit de la mort. *Chroniques*, x. 206.

[2] See the Pardoner in Chaucer's Prologue. A picture striking for its similarity is given in the Vision of Piers Plowman. William Langland's "Piers the Plowman." Edited by W. W. Skeat, i. 6—9.

marked [1], and it still possessed sufficient vitality to be the Bishop of Norwich's chief means of arousing zeal for the Crusade.

The whole machinery of the Church was at his disposal. He himself was special Legate of the Pope, and as such was superior even to the Archbishops of Canterbury and York in matters pertaining to the Crusade [2]. He could rebuke their clergy and exhort their people without their consent. He did in fact issue a mandate to the clergy of the diocese of York, full of reproaches, commands, and threats [3], but the Archbishop apparently showed no resentment at the intrusion. The monks of St. Alban's had reasons for coldness, when they remembered their own dispute with him [4], but they had only benedictions for the Crusade [5]. An anonymous writer, who was apparently a monk of Canterbury, does indeed grumble, and shows that at any rate some of the orthodox did not approve of this method of propagating the Gospel [6]. The heretics under Wycliffe of course opposed it [7], but

---

[1] "li peuples d'Engleterre qui créoient assér légièrement y eurent trop de foy et ne quidoit nuls." Froissart, x. 207.

[2] He was *Nuncius* (Walsingham, ii. 78), while the Archbishop of Canterbury was *Legatus* (Wilkins' *Concilia*, iii. 176). Both Archbishops were at this period *ex officio* Legates (Stubbs' "Const. Hist. of England," iii. 300, 302), but a special Legate's powers superseded theirs in the matter concerning which he was appointed (Hallam's "Mid. Ages," 1 vol. ed. p. 445).

[3] Wals., ii. 78, 79.   [4] See pages 14, 15.

[5] This is seen in the whole tone of the *Chron. Angliae*, and Walsingham's History, both by St. Alban's monks.

[6] *Eulogium Historiarum* (continuation), iii. 357.

[7] See references, p. 42.

ecclesiastical and national opinion generally was with the Bishop[1] and the services of the Clergy were his.

The term Clergy is almost exhausted in modern England by the parochial clergy, who are the vast majority. Five hundred years ago the monks and the friars rivalled them in numbers[2]. We can readily picture the Parish Priest, for though changed he still survives, and his main duties are the same. It was easy for him with his few domestic ties to turn his back upon his parish and go whither his fancy or his interest led[3]. He is happier now in possessing a home cheered usually by the gentler graces of the wife and the mother, and his social rank is higher. Chaucer's ideal Parish Priest was the brother of the Plowman, and three hundred years later the village clergyman still ranked with upper servants[4].

But the Monk and the Friar have passed away from the religious system of England, and their names have now the poetic charm of something that is gone for ever. The statement is not too sweeping that

---

[1] Wycliffe laments this in his tract *De Cruciata*. Polemical Works, vol. ii. p. 605-6.

[2] There were between 8,000 and 9,000 parishes (Stubbs' "Const. Hist. of Eng." ii. 442-3), and probably not less than 1,000 houses of monks and friars, of which about one-fifth were friaries (See Dixon's "Hist. of the Church of England," i. 319, 20). Some parishes were served by monks or friars.

[3] After the Great Pestilence his people were often very poor, and he sometimes had licence to live in London "and sing there for simony," for "silver is sweet." Wm. Langland's "Piers the Plowman," i. 8—9.

[4] See Macaulay's famous description of the state of England in 1685.

no order of men have remained permanently true to a high ideal, no matter what their first zeal. The Monk and the Friar made lofty professions, but their average was that of sorely-tempted mankind. Some were vicious, nearly all were worldly, and a few were doing their best to live holy lives. The parochial clergyman had fewer temptations. He was not oppressed by such heavy vows; his life was more commonplace, and it was also probably more virtuous.

In the famous phrase of Bernard of Clairvaux, the monks were to regard cities as prisons and solitude as their paradise. With the desire for seclusion from the world the Monastery was to be as self-contained as possible. It was built in the country, and though it often became the centre about which a town or city gathered [1], there were few monasteries that did not possess a wide domain, with room both for the labors and the pleasures of rural life. The monk soon wearied of the manual labor that his rule required, and it is Wycliffe's repeated charge against him that he would not work. The other resource of country life pleased him more, and he became famous for his zeal and skill in field sports. The good Abbot of Leicester died in 1377. A father to the poor, the honored friend of the powerful, he served his order well, and died in the odor of sanctity. One of his good works was to procure a Royal licence to open establishments for breeding grey-

---

[1] Probably few appreciate the extent to which this was true. See *Les Moines d'Occident* par le Comte de Montalembert, I. lxx.—lxxii.

hounds and dogs of all kinds. He and his kennel became famous all over the kingdom, and King Edward III., the Black Prince, and some of the great nobles were content to pay an annual fee for the privilege of having him hunt with them [1]. His pious mind, however, was not absorbed in such frivolities, and he used often to say in private that he only pursued them because of the wider influence he thus gained [2]. With minds less balanced, however, they became a snare, and the monk forgot his prayers and shunned his work to become the sporting country gentleman. His tastes and interests were with the landed classes, and like them he became too often the oppressor of the poor [3].

Concealed in the retirement of rural pursuits, the monk did not stand so prominently before the public as did the friar, who was the man of the world among the clergy. No lordly park was at his door; his home was in the city or town where, as St. Francis of Assisi had intended, himself a beggar, he was to minister to the poor and the suffering. His life was free from the stagnation that threatened the Parish Priest. He ministered to a whole district, and his free coming and going was not always agreeable to the Parish Priest, for this spiritual free lance

---

[1] Knighton, 2630-1.

[2] "Ipse tamen saepius voluit asserere in secretis, se non delectasse in hujusmodi frivolis venationibus nisi solum, &c., &c." Ibid.

[3] Chaucer's picture of the Sporting Monk is amply corroborated by Wycliffe and Longland. The unconscious panegyric of Knighton is striking.

was often the more attractive. Some, ashamed to confess their sins to the priest who knew them, whispered them to the wandering friar, who was a stranger, and his absolution was as good as, and indeed better than, any other, if his own word were to be taken. He cultivated the gifts that should make him popular. He could sing a song when called upon. He could please the ladies by his flattery and attentions[1]. In contact with the rich he learned to enjoy luxury. He was housed like a prince sometimes, and too often his only effort was to get money to beautify his cloister. Nor did he, like St. Francis of Assisi, sprinkle ashes upon delicate food, lest he should be ensnared by its sweetness. When moving in good society he dressed well, and paid great attention to refinements of speech and manner. He preached eloquently, heard confession sweetly, and gave absolution pleasantly. Usually not too hard upon the sinner, he could still move an audience by stern pictures of the tortures of the unrepentant[2]. His versatility had its dangers—as the current saying, "Here is a Friar and therefore a Liar," shows[3]. Yet it was not always matter for

---

[1] Both Chaucer and Wycliffe mention the presents to ladies of which he was lavish. See the Friar in Chaucer's Prologue, and "Unprinted English Works of Wycliffe," edited by F. D. Matthew, p. 12. Jewellery, knives, purses, silk, furs, and *lap-dogs* were among his choice.

[2] This sketch is mainly Chaucer's, but Wycliffe and Langland corroborate it in innumerable places.

[3] "Hic est Frater ergo Mendax." Walsingham, ii. 13.

reproach. It caused greater variety of character and independence of opinion among the friars than was found among the monks [1].

Chaucer's master-hand has drawn a satirical sketch of a day with a Friar. It began with a sermon in the church. He was after money for his convent, and he used his most touching appeal—pity for friends who have passed away and are suffering the tortures of Purgatory. Think, he said, how terrible it is to have the body clawed with flesh-hooks, pricked with awls, baked and burned. And then remember that a Mass said in his convent every day for thirty days would deliver from such pains. It was only necessary to pay the price. His harvest in the church reaped, he sought other fields, with him a brother carrying pen and tablets, and behind them a man with a bag. They went from house to house. Give us wheat, malt or rye, cake or cheese, or cloth or money, cried the Friar, my brother will take down your names and you shall be prayed for in our convent. The gifts went into the man's bag, the brother noted the names, and they passed on. About dinner time the Friar took care to be near a house where the fare was good, and sent his two companions on to the inn. The man of the house was ill, and the Friar gently entered the room, laid down his hat, stick, and wallet, drove the cat from

---

[1] See the extraordinary scene at a great council of prelates and lords at Westminster in 1374, in the presence of the Black Prince. Here it was a friar who ventured to declare against Papal absolutism. *Continuatio Eul. Hist.* iii. 337—339.

the bench by the bedside and sat down. The sick man murmured that it was long since he had been there—more than a fortnight. The Friar said, Yes, he had been busy laboring in prayer for him and other friends. But where is your wife? he asked, I saw her in church this morning. Just then she entered. The Friar rose with great courtesy, and, in the manner of the time, kissed her [1]. "I saw not in the church to-day so fair a wife." With this compliment he turned to business. He had come to speak a little with her sick husband. The parish priests were negligent, and had not the art of dealing tenderly with a troubled conscience. The wife said, Chide him well, he was as angry as a pissmire. The Friar's pious mind was shocked. "Oh Thomas, Thomas, Thomas, this is the Devil's work, this must be mended; I must talk with you." The wife asked what should the good man like for dinner. He cared little for eating, he said. His nourishment was the Bible, but his stomach was destroyed by many vigils, and must therefore be indulged. If quite convenient he should like the liver of a capon, a sliver of soft bread and a roasted pig's head—peculiarly dainty food. The wife then told him a bit of sad news—her child had died since he was there the last time. I knew it, said the Friar, who now first heard of it, I learned it by revelation when I was in bed. Within half an hour of his death I

---

[1] "Mr. Grenville (an entire stranger to all) squeezed me by the hand again, kissed the ladies, and withdrew." Cowper's Letters (March 29, 1784).

saw him borne to bliss. So did two other Friars. I rose up, the tears streaming down my cheeks, and with the rest of the convent sang Te Deum. The comforted mother went off to her duties, and the husband was left to the Friar's ministrations. The one thing he urged was that God hears the holy self-denying Friars as He hears no others. Give to his convent and he should have their intercessions[1].

This is satire, but through it we may see the outline of truth. It was the friar who possessed the art to make a cause popular. The monk and the parish priest, however willing, were less capable. It was therefore to the Friars that the Bishop of Norwich turned. St. Dominic and St. Francis of Assisi would have mourned had they heard some of the sermons of their followers; but they could do better than any one else the work in the parishes [2].

It is Froissart's wise remark that soldiers do not live on pardons[3], and the great thing now was to get money. Preparations were made for a systematic campaign by the Friars, and to stimulate and reward their zeal they were to receive two and a half per cent. of its proceeds. They had the twofold function of exhorting and confessing the people.

---

[1] See the intensely humorous Sompnour's Tale, marred only by its coarseness.

[2] Knighton, 2673; Wycliffe's *De Cruciata*, Polem. Works, vol. ii. pp. 593, 594.

[3] gens d'armes ne vivent point de pardons. *Chroniques*, x. 205, 6.

In their sermons they pricked slumbering consciences, at the confessional they named the price of peace. The confessor kept a list of the names and the price to be paid, and handed it to the clerk who accompanied him. The people made their payments to the clerk, so that no money passed through the hands of the Friars. Their integrity indeed was not above suspicion, as the Bishop well knew, and he exhorted them on pain of excommunication to be loyal, diligent, and honest [1]. Before absolution was given to those promising to join the Crusade or to send a substitute, they were required to take a solemn oath that they would carry out their obligation. Then they were absolved, and even though death should overtake them before their vow could be fulfilled they were safe [2].

The Friars were to see that the parish priests did all in their power to aid the work. Many of them were coldly inclined at first, and the Bishop called them to account sharply. They were to urge not only the rich; the poor also—the poor whose hard lot Wycliffe and Langland paint so darkly—should imitate the widow with her mite. But two classes were to have especial attention—the strong who could fight, and the old and infirm, who, as they approached the dark mystery, might be glad of the comfort of the Indulgence. The Friars were to appoint three or four of the most prominent

---

[1] Knighton, 2673. [2] Ibid. 2674.

persons in each parish to aid the Parish Priest and see that the work was done[1].

It was now the beginning of 1383[2], when the Friars began their work. Success was for a time uncertain. The great lords held aloof, and this seemed at first too formidable to overcome[3], while active opposition from another quarter increased the difficulty. The most striking figure in English history at this period is John Wycliffe. He was near his end[4], and now the great passion of his life was opposition to the Friars. In earlier years he had been almost friendly with them[5], but in nearly every one of the writings of his last two years he attacks them. He admired the noble founder of the Franciscans, St. Francis of Assisi[6], and to oppose them more effectually, adopted his idea of sending out poor preachers among the people. He furnished them with sermons written by himself, and now barefooted, staff in hand, wearing only a coarse cloak, these reformed Friars were going about especially in the Dioceses of Leicester and London[7].

The preaching of the Indulgence itself was to Wycliffe bad enough, but to see it preached by the

---

[1] See the ordinances for publishing the Crusade in Knighton, 2673-4; and the Bishop's Mandate in Walsingham, ii. 78, 79.

[2] The Crusade was not publicly inaugurated until late in December, see p. 27.   [3] Walsingham, ii. 85.

[4] He died December 31, 1384.

[5] See "Unprinted English Works of Wycliffe," ed. by F. D. Matthew. Intro. p. xliii.   [6] Ibid. pp. 39—52.

[7] Knighton, 2657-8; Buddensieg, *Johann Wiclif and seine Zeit*, pp. 169, 170.

Friars aroused all his vehemence. When the work was at its height, he preached at Gloucester on Feb. 24, 1383, and declared that of all the bad things ever planned, the Crusade was the very worst. Bishops who thus received money for sins were sons of the Devil, and those promoting the Crusade were thieves [1]. This is vigorous speech, and we may be sure that it was answered by the Friars in no less animated style. Wycliffe himself dared speak freely, for he was sure of powerful protection. His poor preachers, however, could not speak so openly. The Bishop of Norwich had both the will and the power to silence them, and issued special directions that any opposers of the Crusade should be summoned to London. When the work first began some of them opposed it, but they were apparently soon silenced [2].

Wycliffe, however, continued to protest, and wrote a long tract against the Crusade. He used strong language. In those rough days he would not have been understood to mean what he said had he not done so. The two Popes fighting for power are, he said, like two dogs snarling for a bone. The best way to secure quiet is to take the bone away from both, and this the temporal power should do. Christ was poor and meek; but here we have greed and pride acting in His Name. He prayed for His

---

[1] Knighton, 2660; cp. Wycliffe's "Latin Sermons," iv. 34—42; 117—123, &c.

[2] The Bishop's instructions to put down opposers show that they had already arisen. Wals. ii. 79.

enemies, and His word teaches that a Bishop should be no striver; the Popes curse each other, and the Bishop of Bishops strives for worldly power. He taught that worldly means might not be used even in a good cause; His Vicar uses the most worldly weapons in a bad cause. The Good Shepherd gave His life for the sheep and He reproved those wishing to avenge Him; the Popes sacrifice the lives of many others for their own base and selfish ends. Instead of pitying the weak they rob them. Traitors to Christ, Iscariots, Members of Satan, incarnate sophistical Devils, cried Wycliffe, they incite men to fight in the ranks of Satan, and then teach that Christ grants pardon for thus warring against Himself. With all this strong language, however, there is some calm reasoning. The Pope, said Wycliffe, has authority to do only what is approved by Christ. When he goes beyond this his authority is invalid. Men know what Christ approves, for He has revealed it in the Scriptures. When the Pope approves what is condemned in the Scriptures, as he now does, he becomes Anti-Christ [1].

The Friars, however, were successful in their work in spite of these strong words. No doubt political feeling against France in some cases reinforced religious zeal, and made their work easier. They followed their wonted devices. The only condition on which Absolution could be secured was to give to

[1] Wycliffe's Polemical Works. *De Cruciata*, ii. 579—632. The Tract was written after the campaign in Flanders had begun. Cp. his "Latin Sermons," vol. iv. ; Sermons iv., xiii.—xvi.

The Work in the English Parishes. 43

the Crusade, and the more men gave, the more complete the pardon [1]. No one could succeed in this life nor enter into Paradise who did not give. There was a saying in England that those were happy who were able to die at a time when such blessed privileges were being offered [2]. Not only was the authority of the Confessional used to impress living sinners; promises were made for the dead. A preacher was widely reported to have said that at his command angels came down at once and snatched souls from their torments to carry them off to the joys of Heaven [3], and the people were eager to secure the promised aid of St. Michael for their dead friends [4]. Their enthusiasm made possible what at first had seemed impossible [5]. The women were especially eager, for woman's trust is stronger than man's, and whatever the lords thought, their ladies joined in the work for the Crusade. One lady was reported to have given one hundred pounds, the equivalent of quite twelve hundred now. Silver spoons, dishes, rings, jewellery and ornaments of all kinds were given in response to the eloquence of the Friars [6]. A large cask full of gold was collected. Those who died at this season were urged to leave their entire property to the Church for the Crusade [7]. The work was so suc-

---

[1] Knighton, 2671; Wals., ii. 79; Froissart, x. 207.

[2] Tous ewireux, disoient-il en Engleterre, qui pooit morir en celle saison pour avoir si noble asolution. Froissart, x. 207.

[3] Knighton, 2671.

[4] *Eulogium Historiarum* (continuation), iii. 357.

[5] Wals., ii. 85.   [6] Knighton, 2671.   [7] Froissart, x. 207.

cessful that fraudulent collectors imperilled their souls, as it was complained, by going about deceiving the people and forging the name of the Bishop. Their work assumed such magnitude that the Crown appointed a Commission to enquire into the matter [1].

[1] Rymer's *Fœdera*, Orig. Ed., vii. 383.

V.

THE SETTING OUT.

THE success of the Friars' campaign lightened but did not remove all the difficulties of the Bishop of Norwich. It secured both men and money, but the money, given liberally enough, was not equal to the enormous expense of equipping a large force and keeping it in the field. It was necessary to look to Parliament for further help. Meanwhile the situation in Flanders had slightly altered. The battle of Roosebeke made the French masters of the country, and their policy is seen in what they did at Bruges, the most important place in the country except Ghent. The King of France, already feudal lord over the Count of Flanders, forced the people to take an oath of allegiance to him as sovereign lord, to break off all alliances with the English, and do all they could to injure them and other enemies of France. Hitherto Bruges had supported Pope Urban VI., but the people were now forced to accept the Antipope, Clement VII[1]. The religious question thus became prominent. Tournay, which had not opposed the French, was yet severely pun-

---

[1] M. Kervyn de Lettenhove gives the terms which the King of France dictated, printed by M. Leglay from the Archives of Lille. *Hist. de Flandre*, iii. 532-5, note.

ished only because the people held to Pope Urban VI. The war was indeed made a religious war, for Pope Urban had been generally acknowledged in Flanders[1]. The course of events, however, caused a speedy withdrawal of the French army. The weather in this winter was especially bad, and made a campaign impossible. The King of France's uncles were, moreover, anxious to get back to business which they had on hand in France, for among the spoils at Roosebeke papers were found which showed that the commons of Paris were in sympathy with the Flemish cities. Garrisons were left at Bruges, Ypres, and other towns, and Charles VI. marched back through his own country in a manner that recalled the triumphal processions of ancient Rome, and was soon enjoying with childlike delight the pleasure of cutting off sometimes the arms, but more usually the heads, of the rebellious Parisians. The Count of Flanders, too, played the part of the stern sovereign. The Charters which had guaranteed what liberties the Flemish towns possessed were given up to him at his demand, and for the most part destroyed [2].

It is striking testimony to the valor and determination of the men of Ghent that the day after their defeat at Roosebeke, the King of France wrote in respectful terms urging them to submit their disputes with the Count of Flanders to his decision [3].

---

[1] Kervyn de Lettenhove, *Hist. de Flandre*, iii. 539, 40.
[2] Ibid.; Wals., ii. 82.
[3] See the letter in *Hist. de Flandre*, iii. 534-6.

Their spirit was unbroken, and when the first shock of defeat was over they were more resolute than ever[1]. Francis Ackerman was made their Captain-General, and he was soon in England busily engaged in arousing English sympathy and in trying to fit out a fleet[2]. The opening spring saw Ghent active and unconquered, and still looking to England to help drive the French out of Flanders, and secure for the towns the liberty of which some of them indeed were not worthy.

The English Parliament sat from February 23 to March 10, 1383[3]. Every one wished to see an expedition against France. The only question was who should lead it. The "inexperienced priest[4]," as some contemptuously called the Bishop of Norwich, was thought by many not to be the man who could conduct a great campaign successfully and humble France. It was one thing to receive any help that zeal for the Crusade might bring, but quite another thing to put the force in the field under one who was not a soldier; and it was urged that even if a force under the Bishop should conquer, it would not be for the King but for Pope Urban VI. The King of England's just right to the throne of France would thus be sacrificed to the cause of the Pope[5]. The lords in Parliament took in fact the political and military view of the situation.

---

[1] Froissart, x. 184, 5.
[2] Notes to Kervyn de Lettenhove's Froissart, xx. 4; Froissart, 200, 202.
[3] *Rot. Parl.*, iii. 144; Stubbs' "Const. Hist.," ii. 488 n.
[4] Wals., ii. 84.   [5] Continuation of Higden, ix. 17.

They and all other Englishmen were Urbanists, and denounced the Schismatics with almost the vigor of the Pope himself. John of Gaunt, the rival of the Bishop of Norwich, was so full of zeal for the Church, that he was himself anxious to lead a Crusade. In theory it was the cause of Pope Urban that all were zealous for. In reality the Pope's cause was to be helped only in the degree that it coincided with English political aims.

An ecclesiastic, however, could only hope to lead the expedition by preserving its character as in aid of the Church, and the Bishop was strenuous in doing this. He begged that the tax of one-fifteenth granted by the previous Parliament might be given to him. He would undertake with this to equip five thousand men and keep them in the field for a year with no further expense to the royal treasury[1]. There were stormy debates in the Parliament, and his success was uncertain. "It is not lawful for a Bishop to fight," it was urged. "It is lawful," said the martial Bishop, "in the cause of the Lord and of the Church[2]." The custom was to place military expeditions under the leadership of some lay lord who took the title of Lieutenant of the King, and administered justice and discharged other functions of the Crown. No ecclesiastic ever held such an office. It was asked what should the Bishop do about this? What leaders should he

---

[1] *Rot. Parl.*, iii. 147.
[2] *Eul. Hist.* (continuation), iii. 356.

have? He answered evasively, that he would undertake to have the best leaders in England, but he could not name them until the expedition was ready to start. He would submit names to the King, who might choose one as Lieutenant. The Lieutenant would be supreme in the discharge of his own functions, and he in the matters of the Crusade. The Bishop had been posing as the special champion of the Pope's cause, and now the final objection must have staggered him. If the King of France should renounce the false Pope and accept Pope Urban VI., would the Bishop then give up the campaign? The Captain who protested that he fought only on the cause of the Church must have been puzzled. But he was not to be checked. No, he declared, even if the King of France ceased to be schismatic, he would still, as soldier of the King of England, continue the war against him [1].

The party opposed to the Bishop were not happy in having the leadership of John of Gaunt. He was hated by the people, who heartily supported the Bishop of Norwich against him. In the heat of the debate, he made some offensive remark, which reached the ears of the populace outside, and so excited them that there was danger of a riot. When John of Gaunt understood this, he remembered perhaps that less than two years before a London mob had burned his beautiful Savoy Palace in the Strand, and would have murdered him if they had

[1] *Rot. Parl.*, iii. 147, 8.

found him. In fear now for his own safety he mounted, and escaped from the city[1]. His absence no doubt caused the partial collapse of opposition, and the Bishop of Norwich triumphed. The tax of one-fifteenth was granted to him, and the question of a leader as Lieutenant of the King remained doubtful. If no suitable person could be found, who could arrange with the Bishop of Norwich a satisfactory division of authority, the Bishop should have the sole rule. This meant in effect that he had triumphed completely, for the Lieutenant of the King, if he went at all, must go on the terms that the Bishop of Norwich should dictate[2].

The Parliamentary difficulty settled, the work of mustering the host began. Through the efforts of the Friars many persons in all parts of the kingdom had enlisted, and now the Sheriffs gave notice to these by proclamation to make ready to start[3]. They were to muster at Sandwich and Dover[4]. It is difficult to bring life and movement from the still and silent Past. There were the ring of the anvil as the arms were forged, and the quiet or the clamour of good-bye. It was a strange army that was now slowly making its way to the rendezvous in scattered companies along the English roads. The Pope had given permission to the Clergy to join this holy war as soldiers. Priests and monks and friars might go without any permission from Bishop

---

[1] Continuation of Higden, ix. 18.
[2] *Rot. Parl.*, iii. 148.
[3] Rymer, vii. 385.   [4] Ibid. 386; Froissart, x. 209.

or Abbot, and could still draw whatever revenues they had, leaving their duties undone [1]. The opportunity of seeing the world proved an enticement, and there were many Priests in the company now gathering [2]. The stricter kind indeed were greatly shocked at this. The false monks went, says an indignant brother, professing zeal against the Antipope, but their zeal was really against chastity [3]. Society was in a disturbed state, for the upheaval of the peasants' revolt had not entirely subsided, and many restless spirits no doubt found their way to Dover and Sandwich. Like the Crusaders to the East, the champions of Pope Urban were distinguished by a special dress. They wore a white head-covering with a red cross upon it, and had red scabbards for their swords [4].

Meanwhile, the Bishop's final arrangements in regard to his chief officers were to be made. We know him well enough to understand that it would not be easy to divide authority with him. He found the great nobles unwilling to take the Lieutenancy on terms that he would grant. At last, however, by paying a considerable sum of money, he induced Sir William Beauchamp, brother of the Earl of Warwick, to accept it [5]. He made but a feeble muster of other chief men, and secured only one of distinguished reputation. Sir Hugh Calverley was a brave knight

[1] Walsingham, ii. 76—78.
[2] Froissart, x. 209; Monk of Evesham, p. 44-5.
[3] *Eul. Hist.*, Continuation, iii. 357.
[4] Walsingham, ii. 95.   [5] Ibid. 94.

and a good man. The long and desultory warfare between England and France had given many opportunities for the dashing exploits which had made him famous. These and his fervent piety and works of charity call forth the enthusiastic praises of a St. Alban's monk. "The Lord," he says, "was with him, and directed all his works." His simple, unquestioning faith, free from any taint of heresy, made him eager to crusade in the cause of the Church. Once when in command at Calais he made a descent by sea on Boulogne, burned twenty-six ships which lay in the harbor, and then landing his force, set fire to the suburbs of the town. The Lord's hand was to be acknowledged in his success, and with the houses burning about him, Calverley had the Chaplain say Mass, and heard it patiently to the end. He then pillaged the quarter he had taken, and carried off a great booty, including sheep and cattle from the fields, and some of the inhabitants[1]. Though a dashing soldier, he was still cautious, and the Bishop of Norwich could not have had a better military adviser. But he was only a Knight—not a great noble—and did not in any way rival the Bishop's rule. The other leaders were not distinguished. The chief ones were Sir Thomas Trivet, Sir William Elmham, and Sir William Faringdon. John Ferrars and Hugh Despenser, both relatives of the Bishop, were also among the officers[2].

---

[1] Wals., i. 344, 372. [2] Ib. ii. 85, 6; Froissart, x. 208.

The Setting Out. 53

It was now the end of March, and the Bishop, with his chief officers, appeared before the King's Council for some final words. The leaders of the crusading host swore solemnly that they would fight only against schismatics. The King charged the Bishop to wait at Calais for further help that he would send, and until Sir William Beauchamp, then absent in the marches of Scotland, should join him. Meanwhile he was to occupy himself with harrying the adjoining French territory [1]. The Church, too, now gave the expedition her final benediction. The Friars' work was still going on, and was to continue during the Bishop's absence [2], for reinforcements of both men and money would be required. All through their work the Friars had been aided by the processions and prayers which the people had been exhorted to make [3], and now the Archbishop of Canterbury called the nation to support their absent army by interceding ceaselessly for the success of the expedition [4]. An imposing ceremony was held on April 17, when the Bishop received the Standard of the Cross at Westminster Abbey. It was the Westminster that we know, but less complete, and less sacred with noble memories. The grey towers were wanting, that seen from a distance soar almost white in the dim air of London. The multitude thronged to see the spectacle, and the crowd joined in a great procession to St. Paul's [5]. Immediately after the

---

[1] Froissart, x. 209, 10.   [2] Rymer, vii. 393.   [3] Knighton, 2673.
[4] Wilkins' *Concilia*, iii. 176.   [5] Continuation of Higden, ix. 18.

Bishop set out for Dover. Sir John Philpott, a distinguished merchant and intrepid soldier, and others, were arranging for the transportation to Calais [1]. The Bishop reached Northbourne, in Kent, the manor of the Abbot of St. Augustine's, and was waiting there for a fair wind. The final trial, however, remained. In his short absence, the enemies left behind had already been active. No doubt John of Gaunt had recovered from his fright, and returned to London and to his intrigues. At any rate, the Bishop now received a summons to appear before the King and learn his will. He knew that if he obeyed he should receive some check. His foes would have a scornful triumph, and he would be made a laughing stock. He was conscious, too, that he served a master higher even than the King of England—Pope Urban, and determined on the bold course of disobeying the royal order. He wrote to the King that he was just ready to embark, and the cause would be injured by delay. It was his duty to go forward for the honor of God and the King. He crossed the Channel hurriedly on April 23, and waited at Calais for his army to follow him [2].

---

[1] Walsingham, ii. 88; Rymer, vii. 392.

[2] Walsingham, ii. 88; Continuation of Higden, ix. 18; Froissart, x. 210. These writers do not agree in the date of the Bishop's crossing, confusing it no doubt with that of the army, which followed at irregular intervals. Froissart, usually untrustworthy, seems to give the correct date.

VI.

THE CAMPAIGN IN FLANDERS.

THE Bishop of Norwich had his own private arrangement with Sir William Beauchamp, but before the public Beauchamp stood as Lieutenant of the King, and military leader of the expedition, and by the King's order the Bishop was to wait at Calais a month for him [1]. Meanwhile the destination of the army remained undetermined, and it seemed that in the absence of the leader no plans could be completed. The force came straggling in from England, and little by little the horses and munitions of war were disembarked. Part of the army was lodged in the town, and a part behind temporary entrenchments outside the walls. The Bishop waited for about ten days, but to one who was young and eager the delay became intolerable. The King, he said, had forgotten him. Sir William Beauchamp would not come, as indeed in his heart the Bishop wished that he would not, to rival his sole mastery. His conscience began to work. By lying idle he was wasting the money given for the sacred cause of the Crusade. He held a council with his officers. Emissaries from Ghent were in

[1] Froissart, x. 209.

the camp, urging that it would be easy to drive the French out of Flanders, and that the country was prepared to accept the King of England as feudal lord, because of his just claim to the throne of France. The people of Ghent were also in the habit of saying that they alone in Flanders held to Pope Urban, and might, therefore, hope for aid from the Crusade. This was true only in the sense that Pope Clement had for a time been forced upon the other Flemish towns [1]. The council decided that nothing could be better or more honorable than to adopt the views of Ghent and march into Flanders. The Count of Flanders had expelled the English from the country, and though no declaration of war had been made against him, he was still well known to be the enemy of England, and the King of England had undoubtedly intended that the expedition should help Ghent [2].

Calverley had gone off to visit a relative, who was Captain of the neighboring fortress of Guines, and was absent from the Council. All agreed that nothing should be decided finally until he, the most distinguished soldier in the company, had been consulted. On his return the next day, the Bishop summoned him to his presence and explained the plan. The thought of turning aside to Flanders was a shock to the simple mind of Calverley. He could not forget that they had set out on a holy Crusade, and urged that they had nothing to do

---

[1] *Chron. de Flandres*, 233.   [2] *Rot. Parl.*, iii. 154.

with the wars of kings and lords. They were soldiers of Pope Urban, who had given them his absolution, and the Count and people of Flanders were as good Urbanists as the English themselves. Besides, Flanders had had nothing but war for four years, and was very strong. They should go against France. The King of England was at open war with the King of France, and the French were double enemies of the English people and the true faith. The King had commanded them to wait for Sir William Beauchamp. They should do this. Then the Flemings, who had lost their property, their relatives and friends at the hands of the French, would join them, and they should march into France and conquer.

Calverley could scarcely finish speaking before the hot and fiery Bishop interrupted him. Yes, yes, he said, Calverley knew all about campaigning in France, but he knew nothing about other countries. There were rich Flemish towns near the frontier, and as the Envoys of Ghent said, these had not felt the burden of war. They could be taken easily, and the army could wait there for Sir William Beauchamp. It must be admitted that Calverley kept the avowed purpose of the expedition before his mind more clearly than did its episcopal chief, but he was not the man to dispute with his leader, who was, moreover, of high rank and great lineage. So now he only said that where the Bishop went he should follow. There was no path of which he was afraid. "I well believe it," said the Bishop, and the word went out through the town and camp that the expedition should set out on the next day [1].

Readers of history are rarely interested in a discussion of the materials upon which the story is based. Foundations have no place in the fabric of which they are the support. But the various records of this campaign furnish a good illustration of the fourteenth century substitute for modern war correspondence. The fragmentary character of the news that the chroniclers were able to glean is seen most curiously in the order or disorder of the events they report. We send now to the seat of war men with trained eyes whose business it is to see and record all they can; but the chroniclers were obliged to gather information from men with no special faculty of observation, and often no sense of historical order. The knight who rode with Froissart along the road told what he had seen or done, and Froissart wrote the story out as best he could. Some adventurous monk of St. Alban's returned from the Crusade, or possibly a passing traveller entertained at the hospitable Abbey, told his tale to Walsingham, and he tried to make it a readable history. It would be vain to expect that information gathered in this way should be either full or accurate. When the monkish Chronicler told of political or ecclesiastical

---

[1] Froissart, x. 210-14. This narrative of Froissart fits in so entirely with what we know of the political situation, and of the characters of Calverley and the Bishop of Norwich, that it seems on the whole trustworthy.

events, the papers which the powerful Abbey could command access to, were at his hand to prove or correct his statements. It was different with the story of a campaign. The only records were the fading impressions of actors or spectators. The Duke of Wellington advised that no one should try to tell the story of Waterloo. The story, not of one but of many battles and sieges, is indeed a task that the historian might shrink from. Our chroniclers have tried it, and their records of at any rate this campaign in Flanders are a hopeless discord. The order of events is different in each, and the events themselves have so varied a colouring that it is difficult to see a family likeness. The field of the unknown is indeed so vast that there is room in it for harmonies which unromantic history declares impossible. Happily that which she can least hope to know well is also of least importance to her, for the details of a battle, intense in interest to the actors, are of little use to posterity beyond the limited value they have in the records of military science.

We have an amusing contrast in the two records of the setting out from Calais. "The trumpets sounded," says Froissart with his military tastes; "They raised the standard of the Cross," says the St. Alban's monk, repeating what had most impressed his informant. Both no doubt relate what occurred as the crusading army set out on this May morning to attack Gravelines, a town in Flanders fifteen miles distant from Calais. The surrounding country is flat, and at high tide Gravelines was cut off from the mainland by the sea [1]. It had been occupied by the French after the battle of Roosebeke, and from it they had menaced Calais. Now with its French and Breton garrison it could not be taken without a fight. The tide was low, and the English with the red cross upon their white head-dress, and the standard of the Cross floating before them, were able to begin the assault about noon. They first summoned the defenders to surrender to Pope Urban. The defiance was shouted back that they did not hold to Pope Urban, and should not surrender [2]. A bitter fight followed. Both sides were exasperated by the mutual taunts. To kill such dogs was as meritorious as to destroy so many Jews or Saracens, urged the Bishop of Norwich and Sir Hugh Calverley. Those killed in so good a cause should be blessed martyrs. On the other hand, the French sneered at the motley English host as a band of destitute and unwarlike beggars, and promised the people of Gravelines that a French army should soon come to the rescue. Quicklime was thrown into the assailants' faces. Hot lead was poured upon them from the walls, and great stones were hurled down to crush them. But in vain. The English mounted the wall, which was not high, and broke in among the defenders. The fight lasted all night, but now the English were victorious. The defenders hid themselves, or took refuge in the church, a fortress within a fortress, in which the women and children and valuables

---

[1] Froissart, x. 214. [2] Monk of Evesham, p. 45.

had been placed. The English assaulted and took this, and a scene of fearful carnage followed. The fate of the women is recorded in one word, which may have a terrible meaning. They were "reserved [1]," and the male defenders were destroyed to a man. The Crusaders dragged them from their hiding-places, and killed them without mercy. It was strange work for an army composed largely of parish priests, of monks, and of friars [2]. An immense booty fell into the hands of the victors. There were ships in the harbor, great stores in the warehouses, and so large a supply of horses intended for the French army, that many of the Crusaders, hitherto on foot, were now mounted [3].

Some delay was made at Gravelines, to fortify the place and to wait for reinforcements. Meanwhile the alarm of the English advance spread. The Count of Flanders at Lille heard of the invasion, and at once sent two envoys to demand a reason for the hostile entry into his territory when no declaration of war on the part of England had been made. "We have come on behalf of the Lord of Flanders," said the envoys. "What Lord?" said the Bishop of Norwich, quickly. "The Count of Flanders," said the envoys, "he is the only Lord in Flanders." "In God's name," said the Bishop, "we take the King of France or the Duke of Burgundy to be lords here, for they have conquered the country." The envoys explained that the country had been restored to the

---

[1] 'feminis reservatis.' Monk of Evesham, p. 45. [2] Ib. p. 46.
[3] Froissart, x. 214-15; Walsingham, ii. 88—90.

Count of Flanders at Tournay, and that the Count and his people held to Pope Urban, as the English themselves did. They demanded a safe conduct to England, that they might protest to the King of England against the invasion of their country. It was no part of the Bishop's plan to grant the demand. The delay, while the matter was thus under appeal, would enable the country to arm against the English. Calverley's zeal for the Church suggested the answer that should be given. They were, he said, soldiers of Pope Urban, and a safe conduct to the King of England had nothing to do with their mission. If the people of the country would join the English host in the holy war in which they were engaged they should suffer no damage. The Bishop gave the envoys the wily answer, and they retired discomfited [1].

While the Count of Flanders had been waiting for a reply from the Bishop of Norwich, the inhabitants of the country near Gravelines were arming, and gathering to oppose the English. An illegitimate son of the Count of Flanders, known as the Bastard of Flanders, was at their head, and the effort was a hasty one, made without co-operation with the Count, the ruler of the country. The host gathered at Dunkirk as secretly as possible, so as to surprise the English, who soon again took the road with the arms of the Church and the banner of St. Peter, with the Emblematic Keys, carried before them. They marched along the sea-coast, and in the confusion of

[1] Froissart, x. 215—221.

the varying accounts, we may gather that at some place between Gravelines and Dunkirk they met the army of the Bastard of Flanders. The English were greatly outnumbered, but had been in the field long enough to have learned some discipline. The French put the Flemish artizans, who composed the chief part of their army, in the front, as they were afraid of their loyalty. The English archers worked great havoc among these untrained soldiers. They fled, and another scene of fearful carnage followed. The English pursued the enemy into Dunkirk, and killed thousands of them, while their own loss was very light. The clergy in the English army fought with especial bravery, and it was thought of good omen to the cause of the rightful Pope that the battle was fought on St. Urban's Day, May 25th, 1383 [1]. The fall of Dunkirk, which the English now occupied, brought the mastery of the whole surrounding country. The coast from Calais to Blankenburg was in their hands. Nieuport, Furnes,

---

[1] Walsingham, ii. 90—93; *Chron. Angliae*, 356; Froissart, x. 222—225; Monk of Evesham, 45, 46; *Chronique de Flandres*, 234. Walsingham says that 30,000 Flemings and French were engaged, and 12,000 killed, and that only 12 on the English side were killed. The *Chron. Angliae* says that 17,000 of the enemy were killed, and only 7 English out of a host of 5,000. Froissart says that of 12,000 or more Flemings, 9,000 were killed; and of the 2,100 English, 400 to 500. The *Chronique de Flandres* puts the Flemish loss at 5,000, and the Monk of Evesham at from 10,000 to 11,000, and that of the English at 15. There is harmony in the discord of numbers, to the extent that the English loss was light, and the Flemish and French very heavy.

Bergues, Bourbourg, Poperinghe, Cassel and many other places surrendered, or were captured[1]. The booty was immense, for some of the towns were pillaged mercilessly. These successes were not all due to military causes. The towns, oppressed by French masters, were ready for a change that could not make their position worse. The spirit of some of them was base enough. In the preceding autumn they had surrendered their leaders to the King of France without striking a blow, and were only anxious now to save themselves by bowing to the new conquerors.

To see a great part of Flanders at his feet greatly elated the Bishop of Norwich. He called himself the "Conqueror of West Flanders," and wrote a letter to the young King of France that must have stirred the wrath of that monarch's advisers. The Bishop denounced him as schismatic, and the unjust holder of the French kingdom, and called upon him to put away the false Pope from him[2]. In England his success produced high hopes of political advantage. It was expected that the King of England might now be recognized by the Flemings as feudal lord, and the Bishop was first of all commissioned to redress the grievances between the two countries, and treat for peace. He was then authorized to receive the oaths of homage and fealty of the Count and the people of Flanders[3]. The victories produced

---

[1] Walsingham, ii. 95; Froissart, x. 226—230; *Chron. de Flandres*, 234; Monk of Evesham, 46.
[2] *Eul. Hist.*, Continuation, iii. 357.   [3] Rymer, vii. 395-7.

excitement of another kind in England. The conquerors had secured immense booty, and those who carried the good news back to England took with them horses, cattle, and a great variety of other prizes that had fallen into their hands. The desire to rival the good fortune of those now at the seat of war seized a great many people in England. Apprentices and servants in London ran away from their masters, and hurried across the Channel, and as the news spread many from nearly all parts of the country followed their example. The English peasantry were at this time in a wretched condition. Their unsuccessful revolt had resulted in even greater distress for a time, and they were glad to run off to any new field that had promise of some relief from misery. There is pathetic interest in what Walsingham records of their dreams now of an El Dorado, by which mankind have been so often inspired and deluded. If they could but get across the Channel they should be safe from all future want, they thought. But some who did not feel the pressure of want also hurried off now to join the Bishop of Norwich. Companies of monks and friars turned their back upon their cloisters and the protests of their superiors, and went to the seat of war, eager to see something of this new world which had just been gained. But it was a badly armed and unwarlike host which Sir John Philpott carried across the Channel, and was destined soon to come to grief[1].

The Bishop and his officers had now to decide

[1] Wals., ii. 95; Monk of Evesham, 46.

whither they should next lead their successful army.
The more devout spirits among the English were
anxious to carry out the proper mission of the Crusade, and march into France. We may be sure that
Calverley urged this view. But vigorous and restless
emissaries of Ghent were in the English camp urging
that a decisive blow had yet to be struck before
Flanders was free, and that the army should now
march upon Ypres. Some of the English officers,
the fruits of victory in Flanders already tasted, were
greedy for more. The men of Ghent promised a
large army to join the English. Their view at last
prevailed, and the English leaders resolved to lead
their forces to Ypres [1].

The three most important cities in Flanders at this
time were Ghent, Bruges, and Ypres. Ypres lay in
the south, and was on the main road to Bruges. In
the previous year it had surrendered to the French
without striking a blow, and it was from Ypres that
they marched to the victory of Roosebeke. Now it
was held by a French garrison under a brave and
able captain, Pierre van der Zype [2], and the feeling of
the commercial and ruling class in the city was with the
French, while the artizans were said by the men of
Ghent to be in sympathy with the fight for liberty.
If Ypres could be taken communication with France
would be cut off and Bruges would soon fall. It was

---

[1] Froissart, x. 230; Walsingham, ii. 95, 6. Walsingham says that the Bishop went to Ypres unwillingly. There is, however, no trace of this in the Bishop's statement to the King. *Rot. Parl.*, iii. 154.

[2] Froissart, x. 231.

one of the great cities of the world at a time when London had only about forty thousand inhabitants, and was the seat of an extensive woollen and linen industry. The great Gothic Cloth Hall, finished in 1342, with a façade 462 feet in length, is the largest building of its kind in Belgium, and still stands to show how vast was the trade of Ypres in past days. It had outgrown the space within the walls, and was now surrounded by beautiful suburbs more magnificent and extensive than the city itself[1]. We shall be safer if we venture no estimate of its population, but the quiet modern town of less than twenty thousand inhabitants treasures the memory of a past glory which was at its height in the latter part of the fourteenth century.

The alarm of an intended attack by the English soon reached Ypres, and the city adopted vigorous counsels. Each person was ordered to secure a supply of food for himself that should last for four months, and the inhabitants of the suburbs were crowded inside the walls, leaving their rich homes a prey to the approaching enemy. Some of the houses were torn down, and the materials were used for strengthening the fortifications. It was known that the assailants were counting upon support from the populace of the city, and to check this, proclamation was made in the market-place that any one favoring the enemy should be punished with death. All available military stores were secured. Yet even with this bustle of preparation the city was almost sur-

[1] *Religieux de St. Denis*, 268; *Chronicon de Flandres*, 235.

prised by the English. On June 9 they suddenly appeared. The business of a great city must go on even in disturbed times, and the workmen were quietly at their work when the alarm was given by the ringing of the city bells. They rushed to the defence, while the English, deceived by the vastness of the suburbs which had fallen into their hands, fancied that they had secured the whole city. As they penetrated farther they were soon undeceived. An English officer, riding in advance of his company, was shot from the walls, and the gates were shut in their faces. The army from Ghent, under Francis Ackerman, now joined the English in assaulting the town. The people of Ypres set fire to the suburbs of which the enemy had taken possession, and a night of confusion and tumult followed, one of many that Ypres was destined to see in the next two months. At midnight the burning houses made it as bright as day in the market-place of Ypres. The men of Ghent felt sure that the populace of the city would join them, and as the fire raged about the walls they shouted to the people to remember the past ills their masters had done them, and now to kill them and join the fight for liberty. There was no response, and the assailants gained no advantage in this first assault that began the long and disastrous siege [1].

We have the detailed narrative of one who appears to have been in the city during the siege, but he does not attempt any estimate of the numbers on either side [2]. Froissart says that, besides the English,

[1] *Chronique de Flandres*, 234-6.   [2] Ib. p. 234—43.

20,000 men from Ghent took part in the siege[1], while Walsingham declares that there were 30,000 from Ghent and 60,000 from England[2]. These estimates are no doubt exaggerated. The Bishop of Norwich, when he returned to England, was accused of not having fulfilled his promise to lead 5,000 men into the field. His defence was, that before Ypres he had mustered as many as this[3], and if he had mustered twelve times the number he would no doubt have said so. Whatever their numbers, the army from Ghent and the English were able to cut the city off from all outside supplies. The siege lasted so long that there was time for every variety of tactics. The besiegers made repeated assaults, and there were many hand-to-hand fights, with heavy loss on both sides. The stream that supplied the moat was turned from its course, and attempts were then made to fill up the dry ditch and scale the wall. Artillery threw stones into Ypres day and night. The wall was mined; the besiegers tried to set the town on fire. But all failed. The assailants were met by a skill and energy greater than their own, and Ypres at the end of two months remained unconquered[4].

The Count of Flanders, who lay at Lille, was doing what he could to help the besieged city. He induced the Bishop of Liège to intercede with his episcopal

---

[1] Froissart, x. 230.   [2] Walsingham, ii. 96.
[3] *Rot. Parl.*, iii. 154.
[4] *Chronique de Flandres*, 234—43; Monk of Evesham, 46; Continuation of Higden, ix. 21.

brother, the chief of the English expedition, and to urge that the Count of Flanders was a good Urbanist, as the two Bishops themselves were. If the English would march away from Ypres to fight the real enemies of Pope Urban, the Count of Flanders would add five hundred men to their force for three months at his own expense. Ackerman and the other captains from Ghent greatly feared that their allies should be entrapped by such offers. They urged that the Count's promises were untrustworthy, and that the English should stay and carry the siege through, for Ypres must soon yield. The Bishop of Liège at last went away unsuccessful, and the Bishop of Norwich turned with vigor to the work before Ypres[1]. With one of his engines he threw a letter into the town urging the people to rise against their masters. When this failed, he sent a messenger offering mercy if the city would surrender, and declared that otherwise he should burn the place and put all the inhabitants to the sword. Then he invited a deputation to meet him, and received them with great courtesy, and had them to dine with him. The Bishop declared that he, no doubt as representing the King of England, was lord of West Flanders, and therefore their lord. As the people of Ypres still refused to recognize him in this capacity, he decided at last to bring his spiritual authority into exercise. He requested that representatives from Ypres of the three estates should be sent to an interview with him. Four bishops, four knights, and four

[1] Froissart, x. 235, 6.

burghers came to the English camp. The Bishop received them in full pontificals, with the mitre on his head and the pastoral staff and the Crusader's sword by his side. The delegates from Ypres might protest that they held loyally to Pope Urban, but now the Bishop showed them the terms of the Pope's bull, and commanded them to obey him as the Pope's representative. The delegates demurred, and then the Bishop pronounced the final judgment of the Church against them. Raising his hand to Heaven, he solemnly excommunicated them in the name of Pope Urban. The impressiveness of the scene was marred by the prompt interruption of the Provost of St. Martin's, one of the delegates from Ypres: "Please God, my Lord," he said, "you have no power to excommunicate us, for we appeal to the Pope himself." The delegates retired, and the Bishop of Norwich commanded the azure banner of the Church with the crucifix upon it to be raised in the English camp. The people of Ypres, he proclaimed, were now outcasts as much as if they were Jews or Saracens. The display of the banner of the Church caused uneasiness within the walls of Ypres. The people were afraid to fight against a banner that they themselves honored. But the clergy of the city quieted their fears by leading a procession through the streets in honor of the Church, and thus showed their loyalty to the Pope. It was a strange medley of protestations [1].

---

[1] *Chronique de Flandres*, 239, 40. M. Kervyn de Lettenhove gives some details of the interview between the Bishop and the represen-

As the siege went on both sides became greatly distressed. The defenders of Ypres had always to combat the danger in their own camp of a rising on behalf of the besiegers. Soon both food and water began to fail, and it is a singular comment upon the chivalry of the days of chivalry, that the women whose husbands were absent were turned out of the city when the pressure of famine was felt. What became of them we may only imagine. Human life and female honor found little reverence in a rough army of the fourteenth century, and there is a whole tale of misery and anguish in the single line in which the Chronicler notes the event [1].

In the English camp there was discord and trouble. The force was badly governed. No Lieutenant of the King had joined the army of the Bishop of Norwich. Sir William Beauchamp had returned from Scotland and made preparations for setting out with a considerable force to join the Crusade [2]; still some influence not fully known to us, but probably that of John of Gaunt, kept him back [3]. When it was seen that Beauchamp was not coming, the King sent to the Bishop proposing another military leader, but the courteous language of his reply did not conceal his desire to remain sole master of the host, and such he continued [4]. The result was disastrous. However zealous, he

---

tatives of the three estates, which are not in the printed Chronicle. They are no doubt from MSS. Notes to Froissart, x. 511, 12.

[1] *Chronique de Flandres*, 243.   [2] Froissart, x. 233, 4.
[3] Wals., ii. 94.   [4] *Rot. Parl.*, iii. 154.

was still unskilled in war, and his ignorance caused the contempt of the trained soldiers under his command. Some refused to obey him [1], and some of his officers indeed were charged with being in league with the enemy inside Ypres, but this was never clearly proven [2]. Distrust and division produced inefficiency, and the English did not press the siege as the army of Ackerman did [3]. To add to the difficulties disease broke out, and there was also scarcity of food. The unarmed English artizans and peasants in search of booty were now arriving in the English camp in great numbers. They were not combatants, they came only for gain, and they were unwilling to submit to discipline. The insanitary conditions caused by this unruly host were probably the reason of the outbreak of a kind of plague that now attacked the English, and many died. At last the Bishop of Norwich angrily demanded from the helpless camp-followers why they had come to encumber his army, and summarily dismissed them, and forbad Sir John Philpott to give passage across the Channel to any more such. The rude and ignorant host thus turned adrift in

---

[1] *Rot. Parl.*, iii. 154.
[2] *Chron. Angliae*, 356; Monk of Evesham, 47; Walsingham, ii. 98. The Monkish Chroniclers nearly all repeat this charge against Trivet and others, probably in palliation of the failure of their champion the Bishop. At a later period several of the English leaders did receive money from the French, in payment as was claimed for stores, &c., handed over by them. If there had been treachery at Ypres it would have been charged in the Parliamentary investigation.
[3] Walsingham, ii. 98; Monk of Evesham, 47.

a strange and hostile country, wandered from place to place causing disorder and tumult. They were enemies of even their own countrymen who occupied many of the Flemish towns, and the friends of none. Most of them perished miserably before they could reach the sea and get across to England [1]. The population of England at this time was less than two and a half millions, and nothing is sadder than this cheapness of human life at a time when its scarcity might have been expected to give it some value. The sordid misery of these unsuccessful fortune-seekers, driven away from the English camp, finds a contrast in the voluntary desertion of many of the Bishop's soldiers. These had gained their booty, and now fearing days of adversity, they laid their hands on all they could and made their way back to England [2].

The difficulties of the besiegers were now early in August aggravated by news that came from France. The Count of Flanders, unable to draw the English from the siege of Ypres, and knowing that its loss meant that of all Flanders, had been obliged to look once more to the King of France for help. It was not a pleasant alternative to see his country again occupied by the French, but it was his only one. His son-in-law, the powerful Duke of Burgundy, was to be his intermediary with the French King. An assembly of the King and nobles of France was held

---

[1] *Walsingham*, ii. 97; *Continuation of Higden*, ix. 21; *Monk of Evesham*, 46.   [2] *Rot. Parl.*, iii. 154; *Walsingham*, ii. 98.

at Compiègne in the summer of 1383, and here the Duke of Burgundy urged that France should again come to the rescue of the Count of Flanders. The proposal was readily adopted, and it was agreed that a great host should join the King at Arras by the 15th of August[1].

When the allies heard of this gathering army they decided on a last desperate effort to take Ypres. The final assault was made on Saturday the 8th of August. At daybreak the Bishop of Norwich stood before the English army, raised his hand to Heaven, and gave absolution to the crusading host now going once more to assault the besieged city. From the walls of Ypres the defenders saw the army advancing, and each side understood that this was a final trial of strength. The assault was long and stubborn, but it was in vain. The allies were forced to retire[2]; and for centuries Ypres has continued to celebrate the 8th of August with fêtes and processions as the day of relief from her greatest danger. The allied saw that the siege must be raised, and mutual re-crimination followed. The English complained that they had been promised that Ypres should yield in a few days. Ackerman and the other captains from Ghent[3] in turn declared that the English had not pressed the siege with vigour, and that faith had

---

[1] *Religieux de Saint Denis*, 268; Froissart, x. 236, 241; *Chron. de Flandres*, 244.   [2] Ib. 241-3.

[3] At the close of the siege they were, according to Froissart, "Piètres dou Bos, et Piètres le Witre," x. 243.

not been kept by them[1]. On Monday, August 10, the two besieging armies marched away. In Ypres the bells rang out, and the priests led solemn processions through the streets in thanksgiving for the deliverance[2]. Ypres might rejoice, but the disasters of the long siege proved final. Her stately faubourgs were not rebuilt, and she has never again taken her former rank among the cities of Flanders.

The men of Ghent went home, but still planned to carry on the war. Ackerman soon showed by his brilliant and successful daring in taking Oudenarde[3] that he was a capable leader. But the English army had lost spirit. There was division among the leaders. The Bishop of Norwich, still ardent, wished to press forward and meet the French. It was hard for him to admit defeat. He had been so confident of success that he had refused offered reinforcements from England[4], and had called Ypres his property. During the siege the Marshal of Ypres had fallen into his hands, together with the Bastard of Flanders and other prisoners. He had agreed to accept ransom, and it had been paid, but when he learned that the ransom of the Marshal came from Ypres, he had refused to deliver him up, declaring that the money thus used was already his[5]. And when he had learned that the French King was marching to Flanders, he declared that he should wait for him

---

[1] Walsingham, ii. 99; *Chron. de Flandres*, 235; Froissart, x. 243.
[2] *Chron. de Flandres*, 243.
[3] Froissart, x. 256—61; Walsingham, ii. 107.   [4] Froissart, x. 248.
[5] *Chron. de Flandres*, 239.

and fight him [1]. Now rather than retire, he proposed to march into Picardy and to surprise the French by a night attack [2]. Trivet, Elmham, and other officers declared that it would be the direst folly to risk a fight where they should be only one against a hundred, and refused with some vehemence to follow their leader. Calverley, whatever his opinion of the Bishop's judgment may have been, still held loyally to the chief of the expedition [3]. On Monday, Aug. 10, the English set fire to the suburbs of Ypres, in which they had been quartered, abandoned their artillery and marched away [4]. The army divided ; the chief part retired to places in the rear held by the English. The Bishop of Norwich and Sir Hugh Calverley, with a small following, advanced into Picardy. The temporary dash of a skirmishing party, however, could not conceal the real fact that the expedition had received a disastrous check, and was now in retreat. The advancing party was soon obliged to retire. It met no enemy, as the French army had not yet gathered [5]. Calverley recognized that it was his duty to remain with the rearguard of the retreating army, and the Bishop of Norwich now pressed through to Gravelines on the coast, probably that he might communicate with England, and do his best to secure reinforcements [6].

---

[1] Froissart, x. 247.   [2] Continuation of Higden, ix. 21.
[3] Walsingham, ii. 99, 100 ; Continuation of Higden, ix. 22.
[4] Walsingham, ii. 99; *Chron. de Flandres*, 243 ; *Religieux de St. Denis*, 268.   [5] Walsingham, ii. 100.
[6] Ibid. ; Continuation of Higden, ix. 21.

The French army slowly gathered, and early in September entered Flanders. We have long lists of the great nobles who now came with the French King—the Dukes of Burgundy, Brittany, and Bourbon, the Count of Flanders, who had joined his rescuers, the brilliant soldier, John de Vienne, Admiral of France, and a host of others [1]. The army which they led was an enormous one. We are told that 90,000 men advanced into Flanders, and that the army continued to grow. Whatever its numbers, its vastness astonished old soldiers [2]. At Cassel the English made a show of resistance but soon fell back [3]. "On the advance of the French the priests and apostates who had come to rob, ran away to the sea," says a sharp-tongued critic of the campaign [4]. Cassel was burned by the French [5]. A large part of the English army had now retired as far as Bourbourg near Gravelines. Calverley gathered together what soldiers he could, and threw himself into Bergues, declaring that he should hold it until the expected help came from England [6]. Bergues was defended by only a paling and a ditch. Calverley put the women, the children, and the

---

[1] *Chron. de Flandres*, 244-6. [2] Froissart, x. 242, 251.
[3] *Religieux de St. Denis*, 270.
[4] *Eul. Hist.*, continuation, iii. 357. [5] *Chron. de Flandres*, 244.
[6] Froissart, x. 248; *Religieux de St. Denis*, 270. The Monk of St. Denis confuses Calverley with Sir Robert Knowles. Froissart tells a story of the taking of Drinkham and the massacre of the garrison to a man (*Chron.* v. 246). We know that nothing of the kind occurred at Drinkham (see *Rot. Parl.*, iii. 153). What Froissart describes may have occurred at some other place.

helpless in the church, and organized the defence with practised skill. When the French heard that the English were in Bergues they advanced in four divisions to surround the town. It was a pretty sight, says Froissart, to see their army, the banners glittering in the sun, the flying pennons, the shining helmets and cuirasses, and the moving forest of lances. An English herald was allowed to pass by them on the road and enter Bergues. He told Calverley that an army of twenty-six thousand was coming. Calverley laughed. He had seen many French armies, he said, and none that numbered twenty-six nor yet six thousand. Just then the sentry blew an alarm. Calverley hurried to the walls. The vanguard of the French army, including the divisions of the Duke of Brittany and the Count of Flanders, was in sight, and numbered three thousand. "Here are your twenty-six thousand," sneered Calverley, "let us go to dinner." While he was at table the sentry again sounded the alarm, and Calverley again rushed to the walls. The King of France, his uncles, and many other nobles were defiling before the town with sixteen thousand lances. It was useless to try to hold the place against such an army, and Calverley made up his mind that it was time to go. The English soldiery hurried out of the gate on the side nearest Bourbourg, which the French had not yet reached. They seized the abandoned town. The women were sent to St. Omer, and the helpless English and Flemings who had been left behind were put to the sword. The part of the army that reached the town first secured great pillage. Bergues was set on fire and destroyed. The King of France lodged in a neighbouring abbey, and in the beautiful dry weather the French army lay in the open fields [1].

Calverley led his force to Bourbourg, which was on the way to Gravelines. We have a dramatic picture of his halting before Bourbourg and addressing his companions. "We have made a most humiliating expedition," he said. . . . "The Bishop of Norwich thought to have flown if he had wings. . . . . There is Bourbourg. Go there if you like, I am off to Gravelines and Calais [2]." The speech may be apocryphal, but we know that Calverley went to Gravelines, and the army shut itself up in Bourbourg. The campaign in Flanders was at an end. All that the English might hope for now was to get away with as little loss as possible.

[1] *Religieux de St. Denis*, 270-2; Froissart, x. 249—53.
[2] Ibid. 252.

VII.

THE END OF THE WAR.

EVER since the Bishop of Norwich had left England the talk had been of sending him reinforcements, and the irony of events had made John of Gaunt, the Bishop's rival, the commander of the forces that in August were gathering in Kent to aid the Crusading army in Flanders [1]. The bad news of the beginning of disasters soon reached England. The Bishop of Norwich had hurried to Gravelines, and now, when the French began to press him there, he sent an urgent message to the King of England asking that either the King himself should now come in person and use this good opportunity to fight the King of France, or that he should send him help [2].

In those days an English sovereign spent a large part of the year in moving about from country house to country house, living on the hospitality of his subjects. King Richard II. had been married in the previous year, and now with his queen, Anne of Bohemia, was making a tour of the English abbeys [3]. Richard II. was subject to the sudden rages of energy that weak men often have. Two years be-

---

[1] Continuation of Higden, ix. 23. [2] Walsingham, ii. 103.
[3] Ib. 96, 97 ; Continuation of Higden, ix. 20, 21.

fore, when a great host of insurgents had threatened to avenge the death of their leader, Wat Tyler, he had won them by his courage in suddenly pressing his horse forward to meet them, and crying, " I will be your king, your captain, and your leader [1]." He was at a banquet at Daventry, in Northamptonshire, where there was a Cluniac Priory, when the message of the Bishop of Norwich was brought to him. He started up in great haste and rage, ordered his horse, and rode off with a small following, "as if," says Walsingham, "he would annihilate the King of France that very night." He rode on furiously. St. Alban's lay in his way, and at midnight he aroused the drowsy Abbey to get a change of horses. He borrowed the Abbot's palfrey, and our monkish informant adds slily, forgot to return it. He would not stay and rest, but dashed on again in the night, and reached Westminster. Here fatigue and sleep overcame him. He rested, and when he awoke his ardour had cooled [2]. He had no doubt intended to ride through to the coast and cross the Channel in person. Instead of this, he now sent for John of Gaunt. A royal Council was held. We realize how changed the times are when we find it seriously proposed that the young King of England and the young King of France should settle the disputes between the two nations by a single combat,

---

[1] Walsingham, i. 465.

[2] Walsingham quotes Horace incorrectly to illustrate the effervescence of the King's purpose : " Parturiunt montes, *exibit* ridiculus mus." ii. 103.

or, if one fight were not enough, that John of Gaunt and other uncles of the King of England should fight the three uncles of the King of France. Failing this, a general battle was proposed [1]. What the Bishop of Norwich had long dreaded was now done. A Lieutenant of the King in Flanders was appointed, and he was John of Gaunt [2]; powers which had been given to the Bishop were transferred to his rival. It was decided that not the King but John of Gaunt should go to Flanders, and he was to treat both with the Count and people of Flanders, and with the King of France [3]. But he was in no hurry to help the Bishop of Norwich. His army remained in Kent without attempting to cross the Channel, while the Crusaders shut up in Bourbourg and Gravelines by the King of France were left to extricate themselves as best they could.

Sir William Elmham was in command of the English at Bourbourg [4], while Calverley was with the Bishop of Norwich at Gravelines [5]. Both places were now hard pressed by the French, and the English were fighting with the courage of despair. At Bourbourg, when the French summoned them to surrender, they shouted the defiance: "You are dealing with dogs that can only be taken with iron gloves [6]." The French soldiery, wishing to secure

---

[1] Walsingham, ii. 103; Continuation of Higden, ix. 23; Rymer, vii. 407-9.   [2] Rymer, vii. 408.   [3] Ib. 440, 441.

[4] *Rot. Parl.*, iii. 156.

[5] Walsingham, ii. 102; Continuation of Higden, ix. 22.

[6] *Religieux de St. Denis*, 278.

the rich booty they knew they should find in Bourbourg[1], assaulted the town eagerly. The Greek fire they threw caused the destruction of many houses; and stores and horses were burned with them. But with the fire that consumed one third of the town raging behind them the English fought on the walls, and night at last forced the assailants to retire[2]. In the confusion of the varying accounts it is difficult to know how often the attack was renewed. One writer says that only one day's assault was made[3], another that it was renewed for three days[4], and still another that the contest was kept up for many weeks[5]. We know only that the defence was so determined, that the French army was held in check.

Meanwhile, a great disaster happened to the cause of the Count of Flanders. To reinforce the army before Bourbourg he had withdrawn some of his troops from Oudenarde, an important place near Ghent, which the men of that city had long tried in vain to capture. Francis Ackerman seized the opportunity that the weakening of the garrison offered, and surprised and took the place by a brilliant night attack[6]. The news now reached the French camp that Oudenarde had fallen[7]. Other causes besides this blow made the King of France willing to make terms with the English. It was difficult in a country

---

[1] The English had probably carried thither booty from other places.
[2] Froissart, x. 266, 7; Walsingham, ii. 101; Monk of Evesham, 47.
[3] Froissart, x. 267-9.   [4] Walsingham, iii. 101.
[5] *Religieux de St. Denis*, 279; cp. *Chron. de Flandres*, 246.
[6] Froissart, x. 256—61.   [7] Ibid. x. 268.

already exhausted by war to provide provender for so great an army, and it was also difficult to hold the army together. Under the feudal system an army could not be kept long in the field, for the time of service was limited and short. The French army so imposing in numbers was made up largely of the young sons of burghers and merchants who had had no training in war, and succumbed easily to its fatigues. Dysentery and other diseases broke out, and as many as three hundred soldiers died in a day. Winter was coming on, and in its cold and damp the besieged were at an advantage. The English would fight to the death, and to take them would involve heavy loss. Last of all, the French had long desired peace with the English. Reasonable terms granted now might lead to this desired end [1].

The English, too, were distressed. Both in Gravelines and Bourbourg provisions were scarce [2], and the hope for aid from England seemed as remote as ever. Elmham at Bourbourg, notwithstanding some protests on the part of those who still wished to hold out, opened negotiations with the King of France, through one of his chief officers, the Duke of Brittany, whom English help in past years to secure his dukedom had made friendly now to the distressed English [3]. At Gravelines the French themselves made advances to the Bishop of Norwich, and offered

---

[1] Walsingham, ii. 101; Froissart, x. 268; *Religieux de St. Denis*, 286—94.   [2] Ib. 285; Continuation of Higden, ix. 23.
[3] Walsingham, ii. 102; Froissart, x. 268—70; *Religieux de St. Denis*, 286.

to pay him 15,000 marks for his expenses in fortifying the place if he would abandon or even destroy it and retire [1]. A truce was arranged for a few days [2], and at last it was agreed that the English should be allowed to retire from Bourbourg under the protection of the King of France. The French paid Elmham 2,000 francs nominally for handing over some supplies and prisoners, but the transaction justified the charge of treachery against him. The English were to take their baggage and booty with them, but were not to fight against the King of France before returning to England [3].

It was, according to Froissart, a Wednesday [4], probably the 23rd of September, that the English gathered together what good things they could, piled them in carts and carriages, and left Bourbourg. The French soldiers cast envious eyes on the booty they had coveted, and their discontent was not soothed by the taunts with which the English annoyed them as they passed out and marched to Gravelines, only a few miles off. The French took what vengeance they could on any English who had lingered in Bourbourg, and pillaged the town [5].

Many English had now gathered about Gravelines and Calais. They could not enter, for provisions were

---

[1] Walsingham, ii. 103.

[2] *Rot. Parl.*, iii. 155; Monk of Evesham, 48.

[3] *Rot. Parl.*, iii. 156; Froissart, x. 270; Walsingham, ii. 102; *Chron. Angliae*, 356; Continuation of Higden, ix. 22.

[4] Froissart, x. 270.

[5] *Religieux de St. Denis*, 294; Froissart, x. 270.

scarce in both towns and thousands of defenceless people were stretched along the strand between the two places¹. The Bishop of Norwich, shut up in Gravelines, had refused to take money from the French and to abandon the place². Some of his officers, however, of whom the chief offender was Sir William Faringdon, accepted the French money unknown to the Bishop, and it remained in the hands of his Treasurer³. The situation was hopeless. If the Bishop remained in Gravelines, the first act of the French, when the truce expired, would be to massacre the helpless English outside, and he knew that he should be blamed in England for this result⁴. He set fire to Gravelines, and marched away to Calais. Gravelines was utterly destroyed, but the French soon began to rebuild it. It was repeopled from the surrounding country, and fortified strongly as a menace to Calais⁵. The army that the Bishop of Norwich now led to Calais had neither provisions nor money. The Bishop's Treasurer led the Bishop to believe that he had secured a loan from the merchants of Calais to supply their wants. In reality he used for this purpose a part of the money that had been treacherously received from the French⁶.

The Bishop crossed to England as soon as possible. Trouble enough awaited him. The news that

---

¹ Continuation of Higden, ix. 23 ; *Rot. Parl.*, iii. 156.
² Walsingham, ii. 103.   ³ *Rot. Parl.*, iii. 152–3.   ⁴ Ib. 156.
⁵ Walsingham, ii. 103 ; Continuation of Higden, ix. 23 ; Monk of Evesham, 48 ; *Religieux de St. Denis*, 272-4 ; Froissart, x. 272.
⁶ *Rot. Parl.*, iii. 153.

money had been paid by the French for the evacuation of Gravelines had reached England. His own name was coupled with the charge of treachery, and he had reason to fear the anger of the people who had passed from enthusiasm for the Crusade to indignation at its failure[1]. "They returned dripping with blood and disgracing their country. Blessed be God who confounds the proud," says one sharp critic, who appears to have been a monk of Canterbury[2]. John of Gaunt was waiting for the Bishop on the Kentish shore, and we may imagine the stormy reproaches with which the defeated leader was received by the man whose schemes he had baulked[3]. In the mind of every one Calverley was free from suspicion, and no charge was made against him; but the Bishop of Norwich and his other chief officers were accused before Parliament, which met on the 26th of October[4]. It was not difficult for the Bishop to refute the charge that he had taken money from the French. The treachery had been without his knowledge; yet some of the money had been used to buy provisions for his army. Other charges were pressed. He had received a large sum of money from Parliament, and had promised in return to muster a force of five thousand men at Calais, and to keep them in the field for a year. But his muster at Calais had fallen far short of the promised number,

---

[1] *Rot. Parl.*, iii. 152; Froissart, x. 273.
[2] *Eul. Hist.*, continuation, iii. 357.
[3] Walsingham, ii. 103; Continuation of Higden, ix. 21.
[4] *Rot. Parl.*, iii. 149.

and he was back in England within six months from the setting out. He had surrendered without the King's consent places held in the King's name, and he had disobeyed the King in not waiting in Flanders for help from John of Gaunt. Moreover, the disasters of the whole expedition had come from his incompetence and his obstinacy in refusing the military commander whom the King wished to send.

In the sting of defeat misfortune is fault enough in a military leader, but the Bishop had been worse than unfortunate. He made what defence he could, but the angry Parliament, in days ruder than ours, interrupted him with taunts and questions. He became confused and forgot what he should say. A second and quieter hearing proved vain. His ecclesiastical character saved his personal liberty, but to show disapproval of his conduct, he was commanded to say the Psalter for those killed in the war. He had acted as a temporal lord, and in other respects he was judged as such. He was ordered to pay to the King the money received from the French and improperly used in his service, and in the same judgment he was deprived of his resources. His revenues were seized, he was stripped of the dignity of a temporal lord, and was put to fine and ransom at the will of the King. His accused officers were convicted and punished. Faringdon was found guilty of treason, and the others of receiving money improperly from the French. They were all fined and imprisoned [1].

---

[1] *Rot. Parl.*, iii. 152—158; *Eul. Hist.*, continuation, iii. 357;

John of Gaunt with other commissioners crossed to Calais, and at Lalingham, between Calais and Boulogne there were prolonged negotiations with the French. Efforts to conclude a peace were vain, but a truce was agreed to. The English insisted that Ghent should be included in it, and in spite of the opposition of the Count of Flanders, they gained their point. A truce was signed to endure until October 1st, 1384.

The Crusade settled nothing; no burdens were lightened by it, and many were made heavier. Called into action to rescue the true Pope from the Schismatics, it injured chiefly the Flemish people who obeyed the same Pope and professed similar devotion. The influence of single events upon a nation's thought are too subtle for full analysis by the historian, but the Crusade undoubtedly affected English religious opinion. Men's criticism has always been especially attracted by the inconsistencies and weaknesses of their spiritual leaders. When a Bishop laid aside the pastoral staff for the sword, and priests took an active part in scenes of carnage, the moral sense of the thoughtful was shocked, and enquiry into the system under which this could occur was invited. Already there was

Chron. Angliae, 358; Walsingham, ii. 109; and *Upodeigma Neustriae*, 338; Continuation of Higden, ix. 25, 26. The Bishop's temporalities were restored after two years (Rymer, vii. 479), and in his misfortunes he had the sympathy of his fellow ecclesiastics (Walsingham, ii. 141). He lived to go to other wars (Continuation of Higden, ix. 72; Froissart, xi. 361, 2), and to take active steps to suppress the Wycliffe heresy (Walsingham, ii. 189).

rebellion against it. The scornful laughed at the mysteries which the Church taught [1]; and many of the earnest were searching for some freer truth. It is certain that large numbers of the rich as well as of the poor, of the educated as well as of the uneducated, were at this time in sympathy with Wycliffe's new views [2]. The Crusade increased their discontent with the old system, and so urged them forward in the desire for change.

[1] Walsingham, ii. 12.
[2] *Eul. Hist.*, continuation, iii. 355 ; Higden, 2659.

APPENDIX.

The following are the chief contemporary authorities used:—

Rotuli Parliamentorum ut et Petitiones et Placita in Parliamento Tempore Ricardi II. The Crusade was discussed fully in Parliament, and these records of the proceedings are of the highest value.

Foedera Conventiones Literae et cujuscunque generis acta publica inter Reges Angliae et alios, &c. Accurante Thomae Rymer. The original edition of 1709 has been used unless otherwise specified. These public documents throw much light upon the Crusade.

Chronica Monasterii S. Albani. St. Alban's is now almost a suburb of London and a good Roman road connected it with London. The great abbey was a stopping-place for royalty as well as for pilgrims and travellers of every kind, and thus heard the passing gossip. It had long been famous for its historical chronicle.

   i. *Chronicon Angliae ab anno Domini* 1328, *usque ad annum* 1388. Auctore Monacho quodam S. Albani. Edited by Edward Maunde Thompson. Rolls Series, 1874. The unknown author and Walsingham, if not the same person, were contemporaries, and Walsingham modified and sometimes copied this work in his *Historia Anglicana*.

Appendix.

ii. *Thomae Walsingham quondam Monachi S. Albani. Historia Anglicana*, 2 vols. Edited by H. T. Riley, M.A. Rolls Series, 1863-4. Walsingham was still alive about 1419. He was probably in 1383 a young man old enough to be interested in the Crusade. He is careful but prejudiced.

Oeuvres de Froissart publiées avec les variantes des divers manuscrits par M. le Baron Kervyn de Lettenhove. Twenty-five volumes. Brussels, 1877. The best edition of Froissart, that of M. Siméon Luce, in course of publication by the *Société de L'Histoire de France*, has not yet reached the years 1382-3. Froissart died about 1410. His work is inaccurate but still of great value.

Compilatio Henrici de Knighton Canonici Abbathiae Leycestriensis de Eventibus Angliae in Twysden's *Historiae Anglicanae Scriptores Decem.* London, 1652. Only the first half has as yet been published in the Rolls Series. Living at Leicester near the centre of the Wycliffe movement, the author's testimony as to the Friars' work in the parishes has especial interest; unlike the St. Alban's writers he is friendly to John of Gaunt.

The works of John Wycliffe.
    i. The works published by the Wiclif Society, especially Wycliffe's Latin Sermons (4 vols.), and Polemical Works (2 vols.).
    ii. Select English Works of John Wyclif. Edited by Thomas Arnold. 3 vols. Oxford, 1869-71.
    iii. The English Works of Wyclif, hitherto unprinted. Edited by F. D. Matthew. London, 1880.

Cronique de Flandres, anciennement composée par auteur incertain, et nouvellement mise en lumiere par Denis Sauvage. Lyons, 1561. The unknown author gives a detailed account of the Siege of Ypres, of which he appears to have been an eye-witness.

Historia Vitae et Regni Ricardi II., Angliae Regis. A monacho quodam de Evesham consignata. Ed. Thomas Hearne. Oxford, 1729. Cited as "Monk of Evesham."

Polychronicon Ranulphi Higden Monachi Cestrensis. Vol. IX., Containing a Continuation by Johannes Malverne. Edited by J. R. Lumby. Rolls Series, 1886. Malverne was a Monk of Worcester, and became Canon of Windsor. He died some time after 1394.

Eulogium (*Historiarum sive Temporis*). *Accedunt Continuationes Duae, quarum una ad annum* M.CCCC.XIII., *&c.* Edited by Frank Scott Hayden. Rolls Series, 1863. The Continuation is by an unknown writer, probably a Monk of Canterbury.' He is sharp-tongued and original. Cited usually as *Eul. Hist.*, Continuation.

Chronique du Religieux de St. Denys contenant le Regne de Charles VI. de 1380 à 1422 publiée en Latin pour la premiere fois et traduite par M. L. Bellaguet. Paris, 1839. However valuable the Chronicle of this monk of St. Denis may be for the history of France, his account of the Crusade is careless and inaccurate.

The Poems of Geoffrey Chaucer (died 1400) and the poem of "Piers the Plowman," by William Langland (died about 1400).

Other works, contemporary and modern, which have been used are described with sufficient fulness in the notes.

INDEX.

Ackerman, Francis, 47, 68, 70, 73, 75, 76, 84
Anne of Bohemia, 81
Arras, 21, 24, 65
Artevelde, van, James, 20
——— Philip, 20, 21, 22, 24
Avignon Captivity, The, 1, 3, 5

Beauchamp, Sir W., 51, 53, 55, 57, 72
Bergues, 24, 64, 78—80
Blankenburg, 63
Boulogne, 52, 90
Bourbon, Duke of, 78
Bourbourg, 24, 64, 78, 79, 80, 83-6.
Brewes, Sir John, 15
Bristol, 11
Brittany, Duke of, 78, 79, 85
Bruges, 19, 20, 21, 25, 44, 46, 66
Buckingham, Earl of, 22
Burgundy, Duke of, 61, 74, 75, 78
Burleigh, Manor of, 15

Calais, 25, 52, 55, 59, 60, 86—88, 90
Calverley, Sir Hugh, 8, 51-2, 56-8, 60, 62, 66, 77—80, 88
Cambridgeshire, 17
Canterbury, Archbishop of, 7, 31, 53
Cardinals, The, 3—8
Cassel, 24, 64, 78
Castile, 18
Charles VI., King of France, 57, 61, 64, 76, 79—82, 84, 86
Clement V., Pope, 6, 7, 9,
——— VII., Antipope, 6, 7, 9, 45, 56
Clermont, Council of, 26, 28
Compiègne, 75
Cubith, a rebel, 15

Daventry, 82
Despenser, Edward, 11
——— Henry. See Norwich, Bishop of
——— Hugh, Justiciary, 10
——— Hugh the Elder, 10, 11
——— Hugh the Younger, 10, 11
——— Hugh, 51
Dominic, St., 38
Dover, 50, 51, 54
Dunkirk, 25, 62, 63

Edward II., 10, 11
——— III., 11, 23, 34
Eleanor, wife of Hugh Despenser the Younger, 11
Elmham, Sir W., 52, 77, 83, 85, 86
England, King of. See Richard II.
Evesham, Battle of, 10

Faringdon, Sir W., 52, 87, 89
Ferrars, John, 52
——— Sir Ralph, 11
Flanders, Count of, 19—21, 24, 45-6, 56-7, 61-2, 64, 69-70, 74, 78-9, 82-4, 90
——— Bastard of, 62, 63, 76
France, King of. See Charles VI.
Francis, St., of Assisi, 35, 38
Friars, The, 32, 34—42, 45, 50-1, 53, 65
Fundi, 5
Furnes, 63

Geneva, Robert of. See Clement VII.
Ghent, 19, 20, 25, 44, 46-7, 55-7, 66, 68-70, 75-6, 84, 90
Gloucester, 7, 41
——— Gilbert, Earl of, 11

Index.

Gravelines, 25, 59, 62-3, 77—81, 83. 85-8
Gregory XI., Pope, 1, 2
Guines, 56

Hereford, 11
Huntingdonshire, 17

Icklingham, 16
Indulgences, 28—30, 39, 40, 42-4
Isabella, Queen, 10

John of Gaunt, 18, 22-3, 48-9, 54, 72, 81-3, 88—90

Kent, 54, 81, 83

Lalingham, 90
Leicester, Abbot of, 33-4
Liège, Bishop of, 69-70
Lille, 61, 69
London, 41, 53-4, 65, 67
Lynn, 13, 14
Lyster, John the, 15, 16

Monks, The, 32-4, 50-1, 65
Montfort, Simon de, 10
Morley, Sir W. de, 15
Mortimer, Roger, Earl of March, 10

Newmarket, 16
Nieuport, 63
Norfolk, 15
Northbourne, 54
North Walsham, 16
Norwich, Henry Despenser, Bishop of, 8, 10—17, 23-4, 27-8, 39, 41, 45, 47—57, 60—77, 81-3, 85, 87-9
Oudenarde, 76, 84
Oxford, 24

Paris, 21
Parish Priests, 32, 50-1
Peasants' Revolt, 15-17, 21
Pedro the Cruel, 18
Philpott, Sir John, 54, 65, 73
Picardy, 77

Poperinghe, 24, 64
Prignano, Bartolommeo. See Urban VI.

Richard II., King of England, 22, 26, 47, 53-7, 62, 64, 72, 81-3, 89
Robert of Geneva. See Clement VI.
Romans, The, 2, 3, 5
Rome, 2, 12
Roosebeke, Battle of, 25-6, 45-6, 60, 66

St. Alban's, 14, 15, 82
St. Martin's, Ypres, Provost of, 71
St. Omer, 79
Salisbury, 12
—— Earl of, 22
Sandwich, 50-1
Sceth, a rebel, 15
Schism, The Great, 6—8
Scotland, 53, 72
Stamford, 15

Tivoli, 5
Tournay, 20, 45, 62
Trivet, Sir Thomas, 52, 77
Trunch, a rebel, 15
Tyler, Wat, 82

Urban II., Pope, 26
—— V., Pope, 12, 17
—— VI., Pope, 4—6, 8, 9, 18, 28, 45-9, 51, 54, 56-7, 60, 62, 70, 71, 90
Valenciennes, 19
Vannes, Siege of, 11
Vienne, John de, 78

Wycliffe, John, 23-4, 31, 33, 39—42
Wymundham, Prior of, 14, 15

York, Diocese of, 31
Ypres, 24-5, 46, 66—77
—— Marshal of, 76

Zype, Van der Pierre, 66

www.ingramcontent.com/pod-product-compliance
Lightning Source LLC
Chambersburg PA
CBHW030411170426
43202CB00010B/1567